Prayers
for
DIFFICULT
TIMES

© 2012 by Barbour Publishing, Inc.

Written by Ellyn Sanna.

Print ISBN 978-1-63058-661-4

eBook Editions:
Adobe Digital Edition (.epub) 978-1-63409-054-4
Kindle and MobiPocket Edition (.prc) 978-1-63409-055-1

Published by Barbour Books, an imprint of Barbour Publishing, Inc., P.O. Box 719, Uhrichsville, Ohio 44683, www.barbourbooks.com

Our mission is to publish and distribute inspirational products offering exceptional value and biblical encouragement to the masses.

Member of the
Evangelical Christian
Publishers Association

Printed in China.

Prayers

for

DIFFICULT
TIMES

When You Don't Know What to Pray

Ellyn Sanna

BARBOUR BOOKS
An Imprint of Barbour Publishing, Inc.

Contents

Introduction

Give all your worries and cares to God,
for he cares about you.

1 PETER 5:7 NLT

Prayer doesn't miraculously remove life's challenges. It's not a magic formula that whisks our troubles away. Jesus Himself prayed to be delivered from the cross—and yet through prayer, He also accepted that this was God's will for Him. The apostle Paul prayed to be delivered from "his thorn in the flesh"—but when God did not remove this trouble from his life, Paul allowed God to use it to make him stronger. Prayer was the way both Jesus and Paul struggled with their emotional reactions to life's difficulties. It allowed them to transform the meaning of their circumstances, so that what had been a crisis became an opportunity for God's creative work.

Prayer can do the same for us. As it opens us up to God's Spirit, we will see Him working through us and in us. Prayer will bring us peace even in the midst of the most difficult times.

Use these prayer starters as jumping-off points for your own prayers. Many of them are based on scripture. One or two are prayers from the old saints of our faith. All of them can be used as "conversation starters" between your heart and God's!

Abuse

*This means that anyone who belongs
to Christ has become a new person.
The old life is gone; a new life has begun!*

2 CORINTHIANS 5:17 NLT

Abuse is a topic that's hard to talk about openly. Whether it's something that lies long ago in our past—or it's something our friends or we are dealing with today in the present—the shame that goes along with this topic is hard to face.

But God wants to take away that sense of shame. He wants us to understand that in His eyes, we are clean and pure. Abuse tells lies. It says that the abused person is unworthy of love and dignity and respect. God longs to smash those lies with the love and truth of Christ's Gospel.

In Christ, we are new people. He is waiting to help us walk away from abuse—into a new life.

Lord, I know I am precious in Your eyes. I am beautiful and spotless in Your sight. Help me hold my head high, wrapped in the knowledge that I am Your child. Take away my shame. Heal my wounded memories. Create something new inside me. I trust You to do that which seems impossible. Make me whole again, I pray.

Jesus, I know You came to heal the brokenhearted. Heal my broken heart, I pray. You came to deliver captives into freedom. Set me free from abuse. You came to heal those who are bruised. I ask that You heal the scars of abuse in my heart, in my mind and memories, and in my life. Please rescue me!

God, I can't face this situation all alone.
I know You are always with me—but please
send someone else to help me, someone who will
give me support and guidance, who will help me
take the steps I need to deal with this situation.
I'm not strong enough to do this on my own.

I feel so many things, Lord. I feel guilt. . .
grief. . .fear. . .anger. All these emotions
are mixed up inside me. Sometimes I wonder
how I can ever get past them. And yet I believe
that even in this, You are making me into the
person You want me to be. Somehow—even in
the midst of all this pain—You are working
all things together for my good.

I don't feel very loveable, God. It's hard for me
to believe that You really love me. I'm afraid of
being intimate, even with You. I'm afraid to let
down the barriers I've built around my heart.
Help me to trust You.

I know You are on my side, Lord. You want me to
be whole. You want me to trust You so that I can
receive Your blessings. You want to give me the
capacity to walk in Your grace and wrap myself in
Your love. You are the Creator of the world.
There is nothing too hard for You!

In my own power, I know I could never rise
above this. But in You, all things are possible.
Help me to feel safe and whole again. Give me
peace and joy once more. I claim these things
as my birthright as Your child. Thank You.

Accidents

And we know that in all things God works
for the good of those who love him,
who have been called according to his purpose.

ROMANS 8:28 NIV

When an accident happens, we're suddenly struck with how fragile our lives are. There we are, going along like normal, when without warning, something bad happens. Our sense of safety and security shatters. Life feels shaky, as though unexpected danger is lurking around every corner. It's hard to regain a sense of peace.

But God's love is powerful and creative. The same amazing divine energy that made the world is still at work in each and every event of our lives. What seems like catastrophe will be swept up by His power and made into something that ultimately, in some way we may not be able to even imagine now, will bless us and those we love.

True faith in God doesn't mean that we believe nothing bad will ever happen to us. Instead, it means we trust God to use even the bad things for our good and His glory.

Father, Your Word tells us that You
have an appointed time for everything.
From Your perspective, there are no accidents.
You never get the timing wrong.
Help me to trust Your plan for my life.

God, I know Your works are perfect.
You don't make mistakes. I believe
You know what You're doing, even now,
when I'm in the midst of disaster.

Since You watch over the sparrows, loving Lord,
help me to know that You are all the more aware
of the events in my life. You never sleep, the
psalmist wrote, so nothing takes You by surprise.
I rely on You.

The psalmist wrote that You go before me on my path—and You follow after me. That means You were waiting for me there in the middle of what looked to me like such a terrible accident—and now that it's over, You're here with me still, helping me pick up the pieces. Help me be willing to build something new in the wake of this disaster, with Your help.

It's hard for me to go on now, Creator God. I lie awake at night, burdened with anxiety. When I slip into unconsciousness at last, nightmares trouble my sleep. Restore my peace, I pray. Teach me to rest once more in the shadow of Your wings. I know that You let nothing touch me that has not first passed through Your loving hands.

God, my world seems upside down.
And yet I trust You.
The timing couldn't be worse.
And yet I trust You.
I am overwhelmed with emotion and weariness,
as I try to deal with these events.
And yet I trust You.

Dear Lord, You are all-seeing, all-knowing,
all-powerful, all-loving. You always have my best
in mind. And in You there are no "accidents."

Addiction

It is for freedom that Christ has set us free.
Stand firm, then, and do not let yourselves
be burdened again by a yoke of slavery.

GALATIANS 5:1 NIV

Addiction is a form of slavery. It makes us need a specific substance or activity to get through life—to the point that our need is a compulsion that overpowers our other responsibilities and relationships and even our health. We may not realize how big the problem is, but sooner or later, we wake up to the fact that addiction has become the master. No matter what we believe intellectually about God, addiction becomes our real god. We no longer rely on the Creator of the universe for help with life's challenges. Instead, we cannot face stress or sorrow, weariness or anger, without turning to our addiction.

But God wants to set us free. Jesus came to break the bonds of slavery—including the slavery of addiction!

Lord, You know I want to change. And yet again and again, I fall back into the same addictive behaviors. I get so discouraged with myself. Thank You, Lord, that You are never discouraged with me. You are always waiting to give me one more chance.

Father, I can't do this without support. Show me where I should turn. Lead me to the right counselor, the right group, the right program. I want to change. Show me how.

I can't change the people I love, God, no matter how much I love them. Only You can do that. You know how this addiction in my loved one's life hurts me, how much I wish I could do something, how helpless I feel. I give my feelings to You. I give my loved one to You. I give this entire situation to You. I trust You to bring Your healing power to my loved one's life.

Jesus, in the Gospels You said that if I want to be Your follower, I have to be willing to take up my cross each day and then walk in Your footsteps. I claim this addiction as the cross I carry. I pick it up in Your name. I may never be free of it. But I believe You have a plan for my life, and I know You will give me the strength to carry it.

I am so weak, God. But You promised me that
Your power is made perfect in weakness, that
Your grace is all I need. Here, God. I put my
weakness in Your hands. Use it however You
want. May Your grace fill my life.

I know that the Twelve Steps of Alcoholics
Anonymous requires a "searching and fearless
moral inventory." It's hard for me to undertake
such a terrifying task. I'd rather not look at who
and what I am. But, Lord, You also ask me to
examine my ways and test them, so that I can
truly return to Your presence. So give me the
strength and courage I need. I am ready
to be obedient to Your will.

Adultery

"You know the next commandment pretty well, too:
'Don't go to bed with another's spouse.'
But don't think you've preserved your virtue simply
by staying out of bed. Your heart can be corrupted by
lust even quicker than your body. Those leering looks
you think nobody notices—they also corrupt."

MATTHEW 5:27–28 MSG

We all know the technical definition of adultery, but Jesus pointed out that it's not quite that simple. If we take a look at the root meanings for the word *adultery*, here's what we come up with: the oldest meanings of the word meant "to spoil, to break, to destroy." So any time we let something break our marriage vows, destroy our relationship with our spouse, or spoil the intimacy we share, we have opened the door to adultery. Jesus said that even something as seemingly harmless as ogling someone other than our partner could damage our marriage! God asks us to protect married love, to set a shelter around it that keeps out anything that could threaten it.

God, I stayed true to my spouse—but my spouse
was unfaithful to me. How can I forgive?
How can I ever trust again? How can I
even try to rebuild this broken marriage?
Lord, give me wisdom to face the future.
Show me Your way. Heal my heart.

I failed my spouse, God. How can I forgive
myself? How can I ever hope to be trustworthy
again? How can I begin to rebuild what
my own hands have broken?
I pray that You would give me wisdom, Lord.
Show me Your way. Heal me, heal my spouse,
heal our marriage. Give us hope for the future.

Lord, I wasn't physically unfaithful, not in the
way that my spouse was unfaithful to me.
But remind me that I am not perfect either.
Allow me to see how I have failed my spouse.
Remove my self-righteous indignation and reveal
to me all the ways I, too, have hurt the one I love.
Teach us both humility, so that we can
begin to forgive each other.

Help me, Jesus, to accept all the ways I am at
fault. Remind me not to evade my own guilt by
blaming my spouse for my actions. Help me to
be strong enough to accept the consequences of
what I've done. I know that all I can do now is
give the past to You. Teach me humility, I pray.

Loving Lord, how can I get past this?
My sense of security and my trust have been
broken. The intimacy and privacy I thought
I shared with my spouse have been invaded.
I want to forgive—and yet I'm scared. I can't get
past the lies I was told. I don't know how to begin
rebuilding our marriage when I feel as though
I would be stupid to ever trust again.
Show me the way forward, I pray.

Dear God, You know how badly I hurt my
spouse. Remind me I must give my partner time
to grieve, time to heal. Keep me patient. Teach
me to wait—and to stay committed to the future
while I wait. Create a new heart in me, so that
one day my spouse will trust me once more.

You understand us, Lord. You know what we
are facing. You have a plan for us. Your Spirit
longs to lead us forward into a future of hope
and love and strength. We trust in You.

Alcohol Abuse

But the fruit of the Spirit is. . .self-control. . . .
Those who belong to Christ Jesus have crucified the
flesh with its passions and desires. Since we live by
the Spirit, let us keep in step with the Spirit.

GALATIANS 5:22–25 NIV

When we abuse alcohol, our relationships suffer.
Our physical health suffers. We have less energy
for the people and activities we care about most.
And most of all, our relationship with God suffers.

God wants us at our best, emotionally, physically,
intellectually, socially. Alcohol abuse gets in the way
of this. Our deepest connections with Him can only
thrive when we are becoming the people He created
us to be. He doesn't want anything to hinder that—
including alcohol.

Dear Lord, I'm learning that some situations are harder for me to handle than others. When I'm with certain people, for example, I'm more likely to drink too much. When I allow myself to become emotionally and physically drained, I'm also more likely to turn to alcohol. I could use Your help with this, God! Could You remind me *before* I'm in the situation to protect myself? Help me avoid the social gatherings where I'm likely to drink more than is good for me. Teach me to care for myself by getting enough rest, eating a healthy diet, and setting aside time to rest in Your Spirit, so that I don't get to the point where I'm so weak and overwhelmed I can't resist alcohol's temptation. And when I fall, allow me to learn from my mistakes, rather than wallow in discouragement. I believe in You, Lord. Together, You and I can get through this and find a better way to live.

I know You are helping me, Jesus. I believe You are with me. Please send human helpers, too. Give me the courage to let others know I have this problem—and then to ask for their help. Help me to focus outward, on others, rather than on my own situation. Give me a strong network to depend on, so that I can learn new ways to live.

When I'm stressed, God, it's so easy to reach for a drink. *Just one*, I tell myself, *won't hurt*. But then I find myself thinking, One *more* is all right. And then before I know it, I realize I've done it again. I've turned to alcohol as the crutch to carry my tension. When I'm sober again, the stress is still there, of course. I never seem to learn.

I need Your help with this, Father God.
I need You to help me find new ways of coping,
ways that bring me closer to You. When I'm
overwhelmed by life, teach me instead to exercise,
to sing, to call someone on the phone, to do
something creative, to take a nap. Whatever else
You lead me to, be at its center. Use my feelings
of stress as the trigger that tells me: Time to pray.

Setting boundaries is so hard for me, Lord.
I feel guilty whenever I try to draw a line around
myself, whenever I say this far and no farther.
Give me wisdom to know which lines need
to be drawn, I pray. Give me courage to set
boundaries—and then stick with them.

Anger

Stop being angry! Turn from your rage!
Do not lose your temper—it only leads to harm.

PSALM 37:8 NLT

We all get angry from time to time. But the Bible tells us to not nurse our anger. Instead of dwelling on it, the psalmist says that we should turn away from it. Instead, of feeding it until we explode, we are to let it go. There's nothing wrong with feeling angry sometimes—but when we let our anger drive us, when we lose control of ourselves because we're so full of rage, then we're likely to hurt those around us.

Acknowledge your angry feelings. Don't try to stuff them away or deny that they exist. But then give them to God. Allow Him to be the container that holds your temper—and keeps it from hurting others.

Loving God, I've noticed that I'm more likely
to get angry when I'm focused on myself.
I want to be in control—and when I'm not,
even little things upset me. Remind me that You
are in control, not me. My life is in Your hands.
I don't need to feel frustrated when things don't
go the way I want. Instead, I can wait to see
what new thing You will do.

Jesus, why do I get so angry with others when
they don't act the way I want? My own behavior
is far from perfect. Replace my frustration and
resentment with humility and patience, I pray.

Lord, teach me to follow James's advice
(1:19–20): Help me to be quick to listen
to what others have to say; slow to speak;
and even slower to lose my temper. My anger
will never produce Your righteousness in my life.

Why do I get so angry, Father? Your answer points me to the New Testament, where James's epistle offers me a good explanation of my own heart (4:1–2). Soothe those burning desires inside me, Lord, the ones that war against each other. Remove my craving for things I don't have; instead, let me be content with whatever You have given me. Remind me not to shove and push and quarrel with others, trying to get what I want—and let me instead simply turn to You to satisfy my desires, trusting You will give me whatever I truly need.

Strip away my anger, Lord. Let me clothe myself instead with love and self-control.

Jesus, I try to get rid of my anger, but it keeps coming back. My rage is like a dark stain on a white wall. No matter how many times I try to paint over it, I can still see its mark. And then the paint peels off, and there it is, as dark as ever. Show me how to strip off the stain before I try to paint the wall. Show me the source of my anger. Is it because I am hurt? Or afraid? Is some reaction from my childhood being triggered? Am I jealous and insecure? Am I unsure of my own worth in this situation? Reveal the truth to me, whatever it is—and then heal me, I pray. Only then I will I be able to truly turn from anger.

God, remind me that the sun should not go down on my anger. Help me not to go to bed nursing a grudge that will haunt my sleep and get up with me in the morning. Instead, let me value my relationships enough that I commit myself to working through the conflicts that arise. I know You want us to live in harmony.

Anxiety

Don't fret or worry. Instead of worrying, pray.
Let petitions and praises shape your worries into prayers,
letting God know your concerns. Before you know it, a sense
of God's wholeness, everything coming together for good,
will come and settle you down. It's wonderful what happens
when Christ displaces worry at the center of your life.

PHILIPPIANS 4:6–7 MSG

It's easy to be anxious. Are our loved ones safe? Will we have enough money for what we need? Will we do a good job on a challenging responsibility that's coming up? Will our friends accept us? Will we be able to get everything done that needs doing? Will the people we love most make wise decisions? Anxieties pile up around us, everywhere we turn.

We need to learn to transform our anxiety into a prayer. Each time we find ourselves fretting over what will happen regarding some situation, we can turn over that specific set of circumstances to God. As we make this practice a habit, we will find our trust in God is growing. Instead of anxiety, Christ will dwell at the center of our lives.

Jesus, You know that I often have Martha's
focus on life: I'm anxious and harried,
worried about the many details of my life.
Give me instead a Mary's heart. Help me always
choose Your presence as my first priority—and
then my heart will be at peace.

When everything is going well, I'm not as
anxious, Lord. I feel like I'm in control.
My sense of security is stable. But when I feel
threatened or overwhelmed, I start to get tense.
Use my anxiety, Lord, to remind me that
I'm dependent on Your love. Let each nagging
fear be a nudge that turns me toward
You and Your strength.

God, You know my every anxiety. I cast each
one on You, for I know You care for me.

I realize, Father, that I'm more likely to be anxious when I'm focused on the wrong things. Help me to lay up my treasures in You rather accumulating things in this world. I need have no worries about eternal treasures!

Help me, Jesus, to follow the example of the birds and flowers, creatures who never fret. You never forget to nourish them. Remind me that I am even more precious in Your sight.

The cost of anxiety is too high, Lord. It uses up my energy. It takes its toll on my body, giving me headaches and stomach problems. Even my immune system suffers. And meanwhile, worrying about tomorrow robs me of today's joy. Lord, I don't want to pay the cost of anxiety any longer. Take my worries from me, I pray. Let me trust in You.

Anxiety paralyzes me, God. Please set me free.
Allow me to take whatever action needs to
be taken—and trust the rest to You.

Teach me, Loving Creator, to trust You with all
my heart. Help me not to depend on my own
understanding. I know that when I seek Your
guidance instead, You will lead me on straight
paths. I don't want to rely on my own wisdom.
Instead, I choose to respect Your Word; I will
stay away from anything that pulls me from You.
When I do all this, my heart will be at peace—
and anxiety will no longer steal
my body's health (Proverbs 3).

Arguments

Again I say, don't get involved in foolish, ignorant arguments that only start fights. A servant of the Lord must not quarrel but must be kind to everyone.

2 Timothy 2:23–24 nlt

No matter how hard we try, sooner or later we seem to end up in an argument with someone—and most of the time, it's someone close to us. Small differences of opinion lead to hurt feelings. The hostilities escalate. Eventually, we may not even remember what started it all. All we know is that we're locked in an argument, and neither side wants to be the first to give in and apologize.

But God doesn't want us to quarrel. He calls us instead to kindness. This may mean setting our own opinions aside as being not all that important. . .so that instead we can hear what another thinks. It may require that we keep our mouth shut when angry words threaten to burst out of us. . .so that someone else has a chance to speak.

Does it (whatever "it" is) really matter all that much? Or can we choose to make kindness matter far more?

Lord, I know You really don't care how eloquently I present my case; if I don't speak in love, I am like a noisy gong or a clanging cymbal. The love You call me to is patient and kind; it's not arrogant or rude, it doesn't envy or boast, it doesn't insist on its own way, and it's not irritable or resentful (1 Corinthians 13:1–6). Teach me to stop arguing—and instead simply love.

Sometimes, Jesus, I think I'm arguing on Your behalf. Remind me that You don't need my help convincing others to believe in You. That's Your Spirit's job. My job is to simply carry Your love out into the world.

Creator God, use my voice and words to carry Your Spirit's presence into every conversation. Let me practice soft answers that calm tempers, while I avoid harsh words that stir up anger (Proverbs 15:1).

May I use my conversations only for Your glory, Lord. Remind me to seek to bless others with each thing I say. If arguments and cross words pour out of me, how can I claim to be filled with Your Spirit? Your Word tells us that a salt pond cannot yield fresh water, nor can a fig tree bear olives (James 3:12). Cleanse my heart first, dear God, and then my mouth and all its words, so that my life is not filled with contradiction.

Give me strength, loving Lord, to let go of what
I think—and instead pursue only that which will
help build peace, that which will encourage,
that which will please You.

The book of Proverbs tells me, Lord, that if
I churn milk, I'll get butter. . .if I hit someone
in the nose, it will bleed. . .and if I stir up anger,
I will get into trouble (30:33). Help me to walk
away from arguments! And when I fail to do so,
give me wisdom, patience, courage, and
love to deal with the consequences.

Bankruptcy

*And my God will meet all your needs according to
the riches of his glory in Christ Jesus.*

PHILIPPIANS 4:19 NIV

We all know that we are to put our trust in God rather than money. Even our currency reminds us that "in God we trust." In the world where we live, it makes no sense to put our trust in the economy, our jobs, or our bank accounts. And yet, over and over we forget. We start to depend on finances for our security.

And then the economy crashes, we're laid off, and our bank account dwindles. Maybe we make stupid mistakes along the way. We may never have thought we'd ever be facing bankruptcy—and yet here it is, staring us in the face. It can be a terrifying moment!

Even now, however, God is unchanged. He is *still* able to meet all our needs from the unending wealth of His great riches! The Creator of the universe is on our side. He will take care of us, no matter what.

Our money never gave us security in the first place. Only God keeps us truly safe.

Heavenly Father, my personal storehouses
are utterly empty. My finances are a desert.
I am looking to You. Open Your hand and give
whatever it is I most need. I trust You to know
what that is. Send Your rain to water my life.

Lord, remind me of what is most important.
It would be easy to pray that You would restore
my finances, but instead I pray for courage,
self-confidence, and humility: the courage,
self-confidence, and humility to start over again;
enough courage, self-confidence, and humility
to face the embarrassment I feel when others
know the situation I'm in; and the courage,
self-confidence, and humility to believe that
You still have something good for me ahead.
Remind me that Your love for me never wavers,
no matter what my finances are.

Lord, I've made mistakes before. I don't want to make them again. Send me wise financial counselors. May I know whom to listen to. Show me the way forward.

I'm relying on You, Creator God. I'm done with trusting my own plans. Direct my steps, I pray. Let me trust in You.

Father, in Proverbs it says that wisdom, understanding, and knowledge are necessary to financial success (24:3–4). Dear Lord, build my financial house with wisdom; establish it with understanding; and fill all its rooms with the riches of knowledge. Restore my finances in Your timing, I pray.

Jesus, let me not be so preoccupied with my own financial problems that I forget that others are in need. You told us in Your Word that it is more blessed to give than to receive, so may I never forget to give. Even now, when I have no money to share with others, show me that I still have much to give. Let me be generous with my time and energy; show me ways I can reach out and be of use to others.

Remind me, Lord, that others' situations are far worse than mine. You have blessed me in so many ways. Help me to focus on those blessings now, during this time of financial trouble, and make me a blessing to others.

Betrayal

*It is not an enemy who taunts me—I could bear that.
It is not my foes who so arrogantly insult me—I could
have hidden from them. Instead, it is you—my equal, my
companion and close friend. What good fellowship we once
enjoyed as we walked together to the house of God.*

PSALM 55:12–14 NLT

Sooner or later, all of us feel betrayed in one way or another by someone we've trusted. People let us down. Sometimes it's unintentional, and that hurts badly enough. It's even worse when a friend purposefully stabs us in the back. The hurt can be overwhelming. It's easy to feel angry. It's only natural to want to put up our guard and protect ourselves against further pain.

It's far more challenging to follow Christ's example. He, too, knew what it was like to be betrayed by a friend. And yet He never raised His hand in anger, never spoke sharp words, never sought to return the blow in any way.

If we have chosen to be followers of Jesus Christ, then we, too, must find ways to respond with love to those who have hurt us.

Dear Father, help me to forgive those who have trespassed the boundaries of my life—as You have forgiven my trespasses. Give me strength the forgive the debts of hurt—as You have forgiven all my debts. Remind me that I, too, have made mistakes. I have hurt and betrayed others, and worst of all, I have betrayed You.

Lord, make me strong in Your might.
Help me to put on Your entire armor, so that I can resist the devil's schemes. I know that ultimately, this is a spiritual situation. I'm not dealing with flesh and blood who want to hurt me, but rather the spiritual forces of evil. Let me clasp the shield of faith, so that I can stand firm, even now. Armor me in truth and righteousness (Ephesians 6:10–18).

Give ear to my prayer, O God, and don't
hide Yourself from my pleas for mercy!
Listen to me and answer me. I hear the voices
of my enemies, I feel their oppression, and I
am filled with restlessness and pain. They have
a grudge against me, and now they're heaping
trouble on me. My heart is anguished. I'm
overcome with fear. Oh, that I had wings like a
dove and could fly away from all this! I would
fly somewhere safe, somewhere I could be alone
without having to deal with any of this.
But instead, I will call on You, O Lord.
I know You will rescue me. Morning, noon,
and night—all day long, and all through the
hours of darkness when I cannot sleep—I will
express all my feelings to You. And I know You
will hear me. You will rescue me from all this
trouble. Even though my enemies are still against
me, You will keep me safe. I give You this heavy
burden, Lord; I know You will take care of me.
You will guide my path; You will never let me
slip and fall. I'm counting on You, God
(Psalm 55:1–7, 16–18, 22–23).

Jesus, I know You understand how I feel. You, too, were betrayed by one of Your closest friends. And just as I would never focus on Judas's role in the story rather than Yours, I choose now to look to You, rather than the people who have let me down. You're the One I'm following.
That hasn't changed.

Use my pain at this betrayal for Your purposes, Creator God. Teach me through it.
Draw me closer to You.
Deepen my compassion for others.

Challenges

When you go to war against your enemies and see
horses and chariots and an army greater than yours,
do not be afraid of them, because the LORD your God,
who brought you up out of Egypt, will be with you.
When you are about to go into battle, the priest shall
come forward and address the army. He shall say:
"Hear, Israel: Today you are going into battle against
your enemies. Do not be fainthearted or afraid; do
not panic or be terrified by them. For the LORD your
God is the one who goes with you to fight for you
against your enemies to give you victory."

DEUTERONOMY 20:1–4 NIV

We're not likely to ever face an army of horses and
chariots—but some days, the challenges in our
lives can seem just as threatening as any battlefield.
When that happens, we need to follow the advice
given here in Deuteronomy. First, remember all
that God has done for us in the past. Second,
believe that He is the One who will fight our
battles, not us. We can rely on Him for the victory.

Be my strong tower, Lord. In the midst of all my
life's challenges, I run to You.
Keep me safe (Proverbs 18:10).

You are my refuge and strength, God, my ever-
present help in the midst of challenges. Therefore,
I won't be scared—even if the earth gives way
beneath my feet, even if the mountains fall into
the oceans (Psalm 46:1–3). In the midst of all
these challenges, I know You are with me.

I have set You always before me, Lord.
I'm looking only at You. And because
You're there, right beside me, no challenge
can shake me (Psalm 16:8).

Teach me about You, God, here in the midst
of this situation. May I learn more about Your
power, Your love, and Your amazing creativity.
I know there's nothing too hard for You!

You are the Lord of the Universe. You created
worlds from nothing. You formed me within my
mother's womb and brought me into being. You
have been with me, in every challenge I have ever
faced, since I was born. With each new test,
I've grown. You've revealed Yourself in
new ways all through my life.
I'm waiting now to see what You will do next!

The challenge that lies ahead, Lord, is too big
for me. My self-confidence fails. I can't help but
compare how big the challenge is to my meager
abilities for confronting it. My faith wavers.
But I know that when I admit how weak I truly
am, then You have the chance to reveal Your
strength. The challenge that lies ahead shrinks
when I compare it to the immensity of You.
And I finally realize that my perception
of the challenges that lie ahead
all depends on my perspective.
Keep me focused on You and Your power.

Jesus, I believe I can do all things—because
You make me strong (Philippians 4:13).

Chronic Illness

Have mercy on me, O Lord, for I am weak;
O Lord, heal me, for my bones are troubled.

PSALM 6:2 NKJV

When we face a chronic illness, we often feel a spectrum of emotions: anger, despair, embarrassment, apathy, depression, loneliness, confusion, fear, sorrow. We may feel it's just not fair. At the same time, we don't know what to expect next. We want to give up. We want to scream. We long for someone who understands. We wish we could run away. We're mad at God. We want to hide away and never get out of bed. We long for our old lives back.

All these feelings are normal. They do not make us less of a Christian. They do not interfere with our relationship with God, so long as we share them with Him. We will need help coping with this condition—doctors, counselors, friends, family—but most of all, we will need to find God even here, in the midst of our illness. When we see His face, then we can begin to move forward once more.

I am sick, Lord—and yet I choose to bless
Your name. I feel diminished by this illness—
and yet I give You all that I have left to offer.
Heal me, Lord, if it be Your will. Redeem my
life from destruction. Crown me with Your
loving-kindness and tender mercies
(Psalm 103:1–4).

O my God, my life seems so dark. I don't know
how to rise above this illness. Be my sun, I pray.
Rise over my life with healing in Your wings.
Release me from the walls of disease that hold
me captive. Allow me to run free, like a calf that
runs out of the barn when spring comes
(Malachi 4:2).

Jesus, when You walked this earth, I know You
healed all sorts of diseases. People were always
reaching out to You, clamoring for Your healing.
Just the touch of Your robe sent Your healing
power flowing out to those who had been sick
for years. Jesus, I believe You are the same now as
You were then. You are filled with healing power.
If I could only touch Your robe!

I know, Lord, that You don't always choose to
heal those who are ill. Sometimes, instead,
You ask sick people to bear their infirmity.
And yet even then, I believe You bring healing,
the deepest healing that reaches to the depths
of a person's soul and lasts until eternity.
God, I ask You for that kind of healing.
You know I wish I could be free of this illness,
here, now (right now!), in this life.
But give me the strength to bear it, if instead,
You will heal me in other ways,
ways I need even more.

God, teach me about prayer through this illness. I know You do not always choose to answer prayers as we might want. I know that our perspectives are often too limited for us to even understand what we truly need most. And yet I believe You always hear my prayers. You never ignore me. My prayers always connect me to You—and they open up a space where You can work in me. Please work in me, Lord. In whatever way You choose. This is my prayer.

Teach me, God, to accept the reality of my life. I pray that one day I will be healed (whether in this life or the next)—but in the meantime, give me strength to work with what I have right now. Help me focus on all that I still have, rather than on my illness. Let me not shut off myself from others. May I still be useful to Your Kingdom. Help my life to praise You.

Chronic Pain

After you have suffered a little while, he will restore,
support, and strengthen you, and he will
place you on a firm foundation.

1 PETER 5:10 NLT

Life is full of pain. Even babies deal with colic
and ear infections. As we get older, we experience
backaches, headaches, stomachaches. Most of
these come and go, but the older we get, the more
pain seems to linger. Sometimes pain comes and
stays forever.

When that happens, our entire lives may
undergo a change. It's hard for us to interact with
others the way we once did. We may no longer
enjoy the activities we once liked best. Even our
spiritual lives may suffer.

But God is with us even now. And He
promises to restore, support, and strengthen us, so
that even in the midst of pain, we will stand on a
firm foundation.

Jesus, I know You experienced pain. You did not
hold Yourself separate from human experience,
and You died on the cross in terrible agony.
You understand what I'm feeling now.
I can turn to You, knowing that even if
no one else understands what I'm going
through—You truly do understand.

God, this pain has taken control of my life. I feel
weak and helpless. Discouragement, frustration,
and resentment threaten to drown me.
Lord, please show me the way forward. Allow me
to find ways to control this pain. Teach me how
to live with it. Transform it into something that
leads me closer to You, I pray in Your name.

Christ, I choose to treat this pain as a way I can partake in Your sufferings. I believe that when Your glory is revealed to me, I will also share in Your gladness and joy (1 Peter 4:13).

When I'm discouraged, Lord, remind me that today's suffering is nothing compared to the new work You are performing within me, a shining glory that will one day be revealed (Romans 8:18).

Some days, God, I have to confess that I feel angry with You. Why are You doing this to me? Why won't You take my pain away? Thank You, dear Lord, that You are big enough to handle my anger.

Jesus, I don't know how to obey the apostle
Paul when he tells us to rejoice in our sufferings.
I will wait on You, though, believing that
somehow this suffering will produce
endurance. . .and endurance will produce strength
of character. . .and that hope will grow out of
that, a hope that will never be disappointed.
Thank You for pouring Your love into my heart
through the Holy Spirit (Romans 5:3–5).

Lord, this constant pain is a heavy burden.
I cast it on You. Sustain me, I pray
(Psalm 55:22).

Church Discord

There are six things the LORD hates—no, seven things he detests: haughty eyes, a lying tongue, hands that kill the innocent, a heart that plots evil, feet that race to do wrong, a false witness who pours out lies, a person who sows discord in a family.

PROVERBS 6:16–19 NLT

When arguments and division disrupt our church, we may feel not only disappointed but also disillusioned. A church is a human organization, however, and all humans, at one time or another, fall short of what God wants for them.

What scripture makes clear, however, is that God has no patience with church arguments that spill over into gossip and backstabbing, factions and plots, outright lies and ever-accelerating hostility.

Conflicts are bound to happen in any family, including church families. But God's Spirit always seeks to heal and to restore unity. As Christ's followers, we are called to be open to the Spirit leading us. . .to build peace rather than strife!

Dear Lord, make me a peacemaker. Give me the words to say that will build bridges between the groups and individuals who are in conflict.

Jesus, I don't want to be part of the problem within my church. And yet it's all too easy to be sucked in to the gossip and complaints. I find myself *interested*, wanting to know more. . .and then before long, I realize I'm fanning the fires of disagreement. I'm part of the very problem I hate so much. Help me resist. May I never sow discord within my church.

Heavenly Father, season my speech with Your gracious salt (Colossians 4:6). Give me wisdom to know how to answer each person. Let me seek to use every conversation as a step toward peace.

It's easy, Lord, to trivialize the arguments in our church. But this discord is truly a work of darkness, for it diminishes the effectiveness of Your Body. We are called to bear fruit for You—and these arguments are unproductive and barren. May Your Spirit use me to shine light on this conflict, so we can begin to see its true nature. Transform this situation, Lord, I pray, and may it begin to bear the lasting fruit of Your Holy Spirit.

Jesus, how can we claim to have fellowship with You if we're walking in darkness? We're not practicing the truth; we're telling ourselves lies. Show us Your light, Lord, so that we can walk in it. Restore our fellowship with one another. Wash us clean of anger and division (1 John 1:6–7).

God, our church has prided itself on separating itself from the world's immorality. We're not greedy, we tell ourselves smugly; we don't swindle people; we don't worship the world's false gods. And yet all the while that we've been so proud of ourselves, we've let these same sins into our midst. We've been greedy for own way within our church. We've sought to swindle control from others. We've worshipped the idol of power. And even worse, we've done all this under the guise of seeking to do Your will. Give us eyes to see, Lord— and humble hearts that are willing to change.

Dear Christ, I ask that You would help us put away all malice, all lies, all hypocrisy, all envy, and all gossip. Make us like newborn infants, longing for spiritual milk, so that we can grow together into a mature salvation. Let us taste how truly good You are. We come to You—the Living Stone that humans rejected but God chose—and we ask that we, too, be living stones, so that You can use us to build a spiritual house. We would be holy priests, offering up spiritual sacrifices acceptable to God (1 Peter 2:1–5).

Death of a Child

Blessed are those who mourn,
for they will be comforted.

MATTHEW 5:4 NIV

When parents die, their children are called orphans; when a spouse dies, the remaining partner is a widow or a widower; but when a child dies, the English language has no word for the parents who are left behind. It strikes at our very identity as parents, for our job was to give life, and then to nurture and protect that life—and now we seem to have failed.

This is a loss too terrible to be borne, too immense to be transformed by life's relentless movement forward. We may feel guilty even trying to find a way to heal and go on. We cannot believe that life will ever again hold joy or hope.

And yet Christ's promise in the Beatitudes belongs to us now. As strange and impossible as it may seem, His happiness will be ours, for He will give us courage and comfort even in the midst of sorrow. We do not know how to go forward, but we don't have to know. He knows.

Father, did You cry when Your Son died?
Do You understand what I'm feeling now?

I feel as though I've set out on a journey off
the edge of the world, Lord. All my hopes and
dreams and plans are gone. I don't care about
any of them, now that my child is dead. I don't
understand. I don't know where to turn. Help me.

I know that those around me are grieving
for my child as well, God. And yet my own
grief is unique, for the bond I shared
with my child was all my own.
Thank You for understanding
when no one else does.

Time goes by, Lord, but my grief is still here.
I know that others no longer know how
to help me. They want me to be done with
this grieving process. They want me to
move on and be the person I used to be.
But I'm not done with grieving. I will never
be done with grieving for my child. I cannot
move on, because to do so would mean to
leave my child behind. I will never again
be the person I once was. I can't be.
But Lord, I know You still have a purpose
for me. Please reveal that purpose to me.
Use this grief to transform me into a new
instrument of Your love. May my life be a
living memorial to my child. Even more,
may it be what You want it to be.
Give me strength to place
my grief in Your hands.

Just when I think I'm finally getting a handle on
life again, Lord, I'm overwhelmed all over again
with sorrow. One moment, I'm coping. . .and the
next, I'm sobbing. Sometimes I feel too depressed
to get up in the morning. Other days I feel
filled with rage at others, at life, at You.
Some days, I'm swamped with guilt, with the fear
that I was to blame, that I let my child down.
And then there are the days when I feel all
these emotions, one after another.
God, lead me one step at a time.
Moment by moment, I'm depending on You.

Lord Jesus, thank You for memories.
Show me how to delight once more in my child's
life. I am so grateful that You created this special
individual and that I had the privilege to be this
child's parent. Help me trust this child to
You now, knowing that my child was never
truly mine. This child was always Yours.

Death of a Parent

I will not leave you as orphans; I will come to you.

JOHN 14:18 NIV

No matter how old we are when our parents die, we suddenly find ourselves feeling like scared little children. We've never known a world without our parents in it. Even if we weren't close to them, they were still the most primary foundation of our lives. We are linked to them by invisible bonds that live within our very cells, and their deaths can shake us to the very core.

We may sometimes feel as though those around us don't truly understand our loss. Particularly if our parents were elderly when they died, others may expect us to accept their deaths easily. "After all," we'll hear, "they had a good long life." But clichés like that are small comfort to that frightened child inside our hearts.

But God understands. He is ready to meet us in a new way in the midst of this grief. He will not leave us as orphans.

Father, I thought I was so independent and mature. But the death of my parent makes me see how much I need You. Be with me now, I pray.

Lord, I've been trying to push that scared child inside me to one side. After all, I've been a grown-up for a long time now! But today, I give that child to You. Help me to honor that child's fears—and maybe even listen to the perspectives that child has to offer on my life today. Comfort that child as I grieve for my parents.

Dear God, thank You for my parent's life.
Thank You for all the ways You loved me through
my parent, all the things You taught me, all the
ways You've blessed me. I treasure the memories
that I have. Let me continue to learn from my
parent, even now that my parent is
no longer with me in this life.

I feel guilty, Lord. I could have been a better
child. I could have done more for my parent.
I could have better shown my parent my love.
And now it's too late.
Lord, I know I can't change the past.
And so I give it to You. Help me
let it rest in Your hands.

Now that my parent is dead, Lord, I find myself
remembering so many different stages of my life.
The parent who held me and kissed me when I
was very small. The parent who taught me how to
tie my shoes and ride a bicycle. The parent who
taught me how to drive—and who filled me with
resentment when I was a teenager. The parent
I learned to respect in new ways as an adult.
And the parent I watched grow old.
Loving Lord, let me carry my parent
with me always in my heart. Thank You
for giving me this precious parent.

I wasn't prepared for how much this would hurt,
Jesus. Please walk with me through this grief.
Let me allow this grief to teach me what
You would have me learn.

Death of a Pet

Weeping may last through the night,
but joy comes with the morning.

PSALM 30:5 NLT

Our pets are part of our families. When they die, it's only natural that we feel sorrow and grief, just as we do when a human we love dies. And yet this is a loss that not everyone will understand. After all, it was "just an animal." Some people feel it's inappropriate to express sorrow for the death of a pet.

But God created these animals of ours. God loves them more than we do. (How could it be otherwise?) He understands our sorrow when they die. And He will comfort our hearts.

Dear Lord, I miss my pet. When I come home,
the house seems empty, as though there's a hole
in it now. Please comfort me, I pray.

I know my pet was an animal, not a human
being—but nevertheless I learned about
You from my pet. My pet showed me
unconditional love. My pet delighted in my
presence. I never bored my pet nor was my pet
ever too busy to spend time with me.
You showed me Your love through this little one.
Thank You, Lord.

Heavenly Father, thank You for the gift of my
pet's life. I am grateful that You brought this
animal into my life. I treasure the memories,
and I am grateful that they are mine.

Creator God, You were the One who made this
animal in the first place. So now I trust this
creature back to You. I place my pet in Your
hands, trusting in Your love.

Help me find a way to carry my pet's memory
with me, Lord. May I find joy and
comfort in remembering.

As much as I grieve over our pet's death, Lord,
I know it is even harder for my children.
Show me how to help them in this sorrow.
May we together open our hearts to the pain
of loss, knowing that You will be present to
us in the pain. Use this sad occasion as an
opportunity for us to grow as a family.

God, may my children learn wisdom as they
sorrow. May they not be afraid to love again, even
though all love leads to loss. May they open their
hearts to Your creation and to You.

Death of a Spouse

Be merciful to me, LORD, for I am in distress;
my eyes grow weak with sorrow,
my soul and body with grief.

PSALM 31:9 NIV

After facing life as a couple, it's so hard to be alone again. Not only do we miss the one we love, but we're faced with so many practical challenges. We have to deal with a new financial reality. We have to take over the household responsibilities that our spouse handled. And all the while we're forced to cope with these day-to-day concerns, our hearts are breaking inside us. We've lost the person with whom we were most intimate, our lover and our friend.

There is no quick and easy way through this time. Grief has no shortcuts. But God has promised to be with us, always. Nothing can separate us from His love—and He will walk with us, day by day and moment by moment, as we travel on grief's journey.

Loving Jesus, give me strength to deal
with everything that needs doing now that
my spouse is gone. I have legal tasks and banking
duties to take care of. There's the insurance
and endless paperwork. And then there are my
spouse's clothes and other belongings to sort
through and pack away. When I'm so exhausted
with grief, how can I find the strength
to deal with all these tasks?
Lord, I pray for wise and kind helpers
who will walk with me and guide me through
these difficult days—but I also ask that
You would send Your Spirit to give me strength
for all that needs doing. May I rely on
You to get me through.

God, how am I supposed to handle social
situations now? People act so uncomfortable
around me. They act as though if they pretend
my spouse isn't dead, I won't remember either.
They tiptoe around me awkwardly.
Help me forgive them, Lord. I know
I've probably acted the same way to others.
Please send me someone who will let me cry,
who will give me a hug, and who will sit and
listen as I talk about the one I lost.

Oh God, I can't face the calendar anymore.
Anniversaries, Valentine's Day, birthdays,
Christmas. . .they all bring memories and
fresh pain. I miss my spouse in new ways with
the passing of the seasons. I can't help but think,
Last year at this time, we were. . . And I resent
the passage of time, because each day
takes me further away from the days
I shared with my spouse. Lord, I give my days
to You. May I seek You in each one, even
the ones that are most painful.

Remind me, heavenly Father, even in the midst of my grief to take care of myself. It's hard to care right now. Nothing seems to matter very much. But I know others need me—You need me—and *I* need me (as funny as that sounds). Help me to take time to eat healthy meals. Give me the gift of sleep and relaxation. Remind me to exercise, even if it's just going for a walk.

Thank You, Lord, for my spouse's life.
I am so glad You brought this person into
my life. Without this partner,
I would not be who I am today.
Please continue to bless me through the
memories I treasure of our time together.

Depression

The LORD is close to the brokenhearted and saves those who are crushed in spirit.

PSALM 34:18 NIV

Depression is more than just the daily sadnesses that come and go. It's a deep-seated feeling that grabs hold of us and doesn't let go, day after day. It can take a toll on our social lives, our professional lives, our spiritual lives, and our health. Psychologists tell us that depression is the most common of all psychiatric disorders. Almost all of us, at one time or another in our lives, will experience it.

As Christians we may feel we should be immune to depression. But depression is no sin! God has promised us He will be especially close to us when we go through these bleak times. He will be there at our side, waiting to lead us into His joy once more.

Dear God, I am in an emotional desert, a barren and howling wasteland. Shield me, Lord. Care for me. Guard me as the apple of Your eye (Deuteronomy 32:10).

I'm waiting patiently for You, Lord. I know You will lean down to me and hear my cry. You will draw me up out of the pit of destruction, this miry bog of depression where I'm stuck. You will set my feet on the rock, and You will make my steps steady. And then You will put a new song in my mouth, a song of praise to God. Many will see what You have done for me, and they, too, will put their trust in You (Psalm 40:1–3).

Heavenly Father, why is my soul so cast down?
Why do I feel such turmoil? Help me to hope
in You. I know I will again praise You,
for You are my salvation and my God
(Psalm 42:11).

Jesus, thank You for coming to earth and sharing
our human experiences. I know that in You I
can find peace. In this world, I will run into hard
times—but when that happens, I will take heart,
for I know You have overcome the world
(John 16:33).

Blessed be You, God, the Father of my Lord
Jesus Christ, for You are the Father of mercies
and the God of all comfort. You comfort me in
all my affliction, including this depression that
has me in its grip. Use me one day to comfort
those who are going through something similar.
May I pass along the comfort You give
to me now (2 Corinthians 1:3–4).

Lord, You reached down from above. You took
and drew me up out of the deep waters of
depression. You delivered me from my strong
enemy, from this depression that was too strong
for me to overcome on my own. When calamity
seemed to surround me, You held me steady. You
brought me forth into a large place, a place of
freedom and emotional health. You delivered me,
because I delighted You (2 Samuel 22:17–20).

Disabilities

*"When you give a banquet, invite the poor,
the crippled, the lame, the blind."*

LUKE 14:12–13 NIV

The Gospels make very clear that God cares about people with disabilities. The people who are overlooked and separated from the rest of society are the very people to whom Jesus paid most attention. The Gospels are full of stories of Jesus healing people who are blind, unable to walk, or broken in some other way. We never hear of Him looking down on these people as being less important or less deserving of His time. Instead, He treated each one with respect and compassion—and then He raised them up, so that they could take their place in society once more.

As Christ's followers, we, too, are called to reach out to those with disabilities. We cannot heal their physical issues—but we can treat them with dignity and respect. We can make sure they are not overlooked or ignored. And we can work to bring them back into society, allowing them to contribute to our communities.

You told the apostle Paul, Lord, that Your grace
was all he needed. Your power, You said, is
made perfect in weakness (2 Corinthians 12:9).
Remind me to never look down on any
form of disability as being weakness.
Instead, let me always be open to Your
power working in surprising ways.

Ultimately, Lord, I know that all of us, sooner or
later, will likely encounter some form of disability,
especially as we grow older. Disability is part of
the human condition. I cannot separate myself
from it. Instead, dear God, I pray that You
will use my disabilities for Your glory.

Jesus, I read in the Gospels how You went around restoring people's vision, giving back the ability to walk, allowing the deaf to hear, and healing every disability You encountered. I know it's not likely I can literally heal physical disabilities in the people I meet—but I pray that, nevertheless, Your healing power would work through me.

Dear Father, may I see You in each person,
no matter how broken they may appear to be on
the outside. May I remember that when I serve
those who are disabled, I am truly serving You.

Dealing with this disability takes all my strength,
Lord. I'm exhausted. I don't have anything left to
give to anyone else. Renew my heart, I pray.

Disappointment

Though the fig tree does not bud and there are no grapes on the vines, though the olive crop fails and the fields produce no food, though there are no sheep in the pen and no cattle in the stalls, yet I will rejoice in the LORD, I will be joyful in God my Savior.

HABAKKUK 3:17–18 NIV

Disappointment comes in all shapes and sizes. Maybe life itself has disappointed us. We had hoped to reach a particular milestone by this point in our life—and it hasn't materialized as we'd imagined. In fact, our goal is as far away as ever. We may have had to face that we will never attain it at all. Maybe someone we counted on has let us down, and we're disappointed that this individual is not the person we had thought. Or maybe it's our own selves that have disappointed us. Our own failures and weaknesses have forced us to realize that we're not the people we dreamed of being.

But one thing is certain: no matter what else disappoints us, God never will! When everything else lets us down—when the fig tree doesn't bud, the vines have no grapes, our crops fail, and everything in our lives is empty—we can still rejoice in God our Savior.

Lord, You know how disappointed I feel right now. Remind me, Lord, that I am Your child, and You have a lesson You want me to learn from all this. Help me not to lose heart. I know that even this disappointment comes to me through Your loving hand, because I am Your child. Just as my human parents had to say no to me sometimes, so that I could learn, You, too, are doing what is best for me. You are doing this so that I can grow more like You, so that I can share in Your wholeness. This isn't fun, Lord; in fact, it hurts! But I believe that down the road a ways, I will reap a harvest of peace and righteousness from this disappointment I'm experiencing now (Hebrews 12:5–11).

Jesus, help me to see the joy hidden inside this disappointment. I know that this testing of my faith will help me to develop the ability to persevere—and that ability in turn will allow me to grow up in You and become complete, not lacking anything (James 1:2–4).

God, I'm not the only one to be disappointed. When I look at the Bible, I see person after person who hoped for something—and then was disappointed. Abraham, Moses, David, the prophets, they all learned that disappointment is only temporary. What looks like a loss from my perspective now will one day be revealed as only the next step toward the amazing thing You were doing all along.

Dear Jesus, whenever I cling to circumstances
or people as my only happiness,
I'm bound to be disappointed in the end.
Help me to trust in You instead.

Lord, I'm realizing that when I reach the point
where I have nothing left but You, I can
finally realize that You alone are enough.
All my questions won't be answered in this life.
My circumstances may not be improved. I'll have
to let go of some of the things I've set my heart
on. But none of that matters. You are the
strength of my heart and my portion forever.

Dishonesty

*"I am the way, the truth, and the life.
No one can come to the Father except through me."*

JOHN 14:6 NLT

As Christ's followers, we are to walk in the truth
(3 John 3), love the truth, and believe the truth
(2 Thessalonians 2:10, 12). We are to speak the
truth in love (Ephesians 4:15). Christ came to us
full of grace and truth (John 1:14), but He went still
further than that: He told us that He *is* the truth
personified, the truth incarnate. We are to love the
truth because it is Jesus. We are to stay close to
it and follow after it, because that is the way we
follow our Lord. If we are Christ's representatives,
then those around us should know we always
speak the truth.

Loving Lord, I hate to admit this, but being
honest isn't always easy for me. Little lies slip
out of my mouth so glibly. I don't even think
about them ahead of time. I tell myself they don't
matter. After all, I'm not lying about *big* things.
I'm only lying about trivial things, to make my
life easier, to smooth over awkwardness, to let me
have my way without upsetting anyone.
Lord Jesus, remind me that You are truth.
Teach me that lying hurts Your Spirit.
Help me to love the truth.

Father, sometimes I not only lie to others with
my words; I also lie to myself in my thoughts.
I criticize myself unjustly. Or I go to the other
extreme and excuse myself too easily.
I hide unpleasant truths away where
I don't have to look at them.
Reveal the truth within me, God. Give me
the courage to be honest even with myself.

Lord, help me not to lie to anyone. Instead, give me the strength to shed my old self with its deceitful habits and instead put on the new self You have called me to put on. Renew in me the image of my Creator, so that I may become the true self You always wanted me to be (Colossians 3:9–10).

Remind me, Lord, that if I'm dishonest even in little ways, I am also dishonest in big ways. Help me to be faithful with the smallest things, so that people can count on me to be faithful with life's greatest things (Luke 16:10).

Holy Spirit, lead me into the truth. Help me to act in truth and abide in truth (John 3:21). May the belt of truth hold together my spiritual armor (Ephesians 6:14), protecting me always.

God, I know You never lie, for You are the God of truth. I can trust You to never be dishonest with me. You always keep Your promises. But Your Son called Satan a "liar and the father of lie (John 8:44 niv). Remind me always that when I speak the truth, I am speaking Your Son's language—but when I am dishonest, when I mislead others anyway, I am speaking the language of my enemy.

Distrust

I will trust and not be afraid.

ISAIAH 12:2 NIV

Trust is essential to our psychological well-being. We first learned to trust as babies cared for by loving parents. That most basic level of trust was the foundation on which all our human relationships were built. It is also what makes us able to trust God.

But sometimes parents fail to teach their children how to trust. If our parents hurt us, we may not be able to trust others, including God. Or maybe a close friend or a spouse damaged our trust later in life. When someone who is important to us lets us down, we learn to distrust others. We find it hard to trust even God. We are constantly on guard, trying to protect ourselves against hurt.

God wants to heal our distrust. He knows we can never be whole until we can trust Him. We will never have intimacy—even with God—until we can learn to trust once more.

God, my trust has been shattered. My distrust is
a wound that lurks in the very basement of my
heart. On the outside, I look like I'm okay.
I can laugh and have a good time.
I can even love. But I can't trust.
Lord, clean out the basement of my heart.
Help me to trust.

I want to trust You, God. But I can't.
I want to give You control over my life.
But no matter how many times I say the words,
I can't follow through on them. I feel stuck.
I'm helpless to change.
Lord, I know You can do the impossible.
Work a miracle in my heart, I pray.

I keep saying that I love You, Lord. But I realize now that love and trust go together. I can't truly love You until I trust You. And without trust, I will never truly experience Your love for me.

When I read the Bible, I see, dear God, that I'm not the only one who had this problem. Trust was just as hard for many of the great Bible heroes. Jonah, for example, ended up inside a big fish because he couldn't trust Your commands. Father, thank You that You never abandon me, even when I fail to trust You. Even when I find myself inside life's "big fish," You are there with me. And just as You did with Jonah, You give me another chance.

God, You are the One who began a good work in
me (Philippians 1:6)—and I know You will not
walk away from me now. You will help me
to grow in Your grace. . .until I learn
to trust You absolutely.

Lord, I do trust You.
But help me to trust You more.

Divorce/Separation

There is no God like you in the skies above or on the earth below, who unswervingly keeps covenant with his servants and unfailingly loves them.

2 CHRONICLES 6:14 MSG

When a marriage fails, it hurts. Even if the relationship itself was damaged and unhealthy, the final breakup is painful. It forces us to face the loss of our dreams and hopes. We are full of disappointment and sorrow. And on top of that, we face new stress and responsibilities. Our routines and responsibilities have been disrupted and rearranged. Our relationships with others—children, extended family, friends, church members—may have been shaken as well. We may feel embarrassment and resentment alongside our sorrow and hurt. The future we had hoped for is gone, and we don't know what to hope for in its place.

All we can do is turn to God. In the midst of what seems like one of the biggest failures of our lives, He is there. He has not abandoned us. He still has plans for our lives. And His love for us will never fail.

Dear Jesus, I feel so many things all at the same time. I'm furious and sad, exhausted and frustrated, confused and relieved. Some days I don't feel anything at all, only numbness. Other days I'm filled with anxiety about the future. And then there are the days when I can't stop crying. Thank You that whatever I'm feeling, You're always there with me. You understand me even when I don't understand myself.

My heavenly Father, thank You for Your patience with me during this time. I just don't seem to be able to live up to my usual standards right now. I can't get as much as done. I seem to have less energy. I don't feel like I'm much use to You or Your Kingdom.
Lord, one day make me useful again.
In the meantime, I'll let myself drop into Your hands. Please don't let me fall!

Dear Jesus, I don't want to swallow my anger and hurt so that they fester inside me—but I also don't want to get stuck in them. I've gone over the past so many times, examining each mistake and hurt from every possible perspective. Help me to know when it's time to let it go—and move on into whatever You have for me next.

Sometimes, Creator God, I feel as though my future died when my marriage did. I feel guilty even hoping to replace those old dreams with new ones. Help me to trust You. Help me to believe that You still have dreams for my life.

Lord, I don't know how to move forward. I think
I need help. Show me where to turn. Give me
discernment to know if I need to talk to a wise
friend—or if I need professional counseling to
help me deal with this. Guide me to the right
person who will shed Your light on my life.

I'm grieving today, Lord—grieving for the loss of
companionship in my life, for the death of hopes,
for broken promises, and for plans that will
never be fulfilled. The pain I feel scares me.
I'm afraid I can never recover from this wound.
Give me courage to mourn my marriage.
Give me strength to place it in
Your loving hands and leave it there.
Give me hope again. Heal my heart, I pray.

Doubt

Jesus immediately reached out and grabbed him.
"You have so little faith," Jesus said.
"Why did you doubt me?"

MATTHEW 14:31 NLT

Peter was walking along on the surface of the water, his eyes fixed on Jesus, doing just fine. Suddenly, he realized what he was doing. He looked at the waves beneath his feet, and he knew that what he was doing was *impossible*. Instantly, his feet sank into the water. He knew he was going to drown.

But Jesus didn't let him. Our Lord grabbed His good friend and saved him. And He does the same for us, over and over, every time we're swamped with doubts and start to sink into life's depths. "Why do you doubt Me?" He asks us. "Have I *ever* let you sink?"

Jesus, I can't help but identify with Peter—and with Thomas, too. I want *proof* that You will keep Your promises to me, that You are who You say are, that You will help me to do the things that seem so impossible. Forgive me for doubting You.

Lord, fill me with Your wisdom—the wisdom that is wholehearted and straightforward, free from wavering and doubts (James 3:17).

Holy Spirit, I pray for the assurance of things hoped for, the conviction of things not seen. By faith, I understand that God created the universe by His Word, so that the visible world was made out of things that cannot be seen. I know that by faith Abel gave You the sacrifice You desired, while Cain, because of his lack of faith, did not. Because of Abel's faith, I still hear his voice speaking to me in the scripture. Because of Enoch's faith, You took him to You, allowing him to skip over death. If Noah had been full of doubts, he would never have built the ark. Abraham and Sarah, Isaac and Jacob, they all had doubts—and yet they all surrendered their doubts to You and walked in faith, doing the impossible. Lord, help me to do the same (Hebrews 11:1–12).

Dearest Christ, thank You for Your Body. Thank You that those who are strong in Your Body help carry me when I am weak. When I am full of doubt, I rely on their faith. Give me strength one day to do the same for someone else.

God, You know I still have doubts. But despite my doubts, I affirm that neither life nor death, neither angels nor any spiritual power, neither height nor depth, nothing the future holds— in fact, nothing whatsoever will ever be able to separate me from Your love (Romans 8:38–39)!

Drug Abuse

Do you not know that your bodies are temples
of the Holy Spirit, who is in you,
whom you have received from God?
You are not your own; you were bought at a price.
Therefore honor God with your bodies.

1 CORINTHIANS 6:19–20 NIV

Our bodies are the Holy Spirit's sanctuary. We've heard that so many times that we seldom think about what it truly means. God's Spirit lives inside us! He has chosen our flesh and blood as the place from which He shines. And not only that—Christ died on the cross so that nothing would stand in the way of God's Spirit within us.

When we consider all that, why would we want to do anything that would dim the Spirit's light? Abusing drugs is dangerous to both our bodies and our spirits. God wants both to shine with His light.

Lord, keep me sober-minded and on my guard.
I know that the enemy of my soul prowls around
like a hungry lion, looking to eat me alive.
I believe that if I can stand firm,
You will make me whole and strong
(1 Peter 5:8–11).

God, I know You're not a goody-goody!
You don't make rules simply for the sake of
making them. In fact, I can say along with
the apostle Paul, "I am allowed to do anything"
(1 Corinthians 6:12 NLT). But even though all
things are allowed, not everything is helpful or
productive. I refuse to be enslaved by anything.

Jesus, You called me to freedom. I don't want to use that freedom for something that will lead me away from You. Instead, help me to always use Your freedom to serve others (Galatians 5:13).

Creator God, You want me to be this world's "salt." You have called me to be a light. Drug abuse robs my salt of its savor. It knocks my light off its stand and instead, it puts a bushel over it, so that no one can see it. Make me truly "salty," God! Let my light shine so that everyone can see it. Be glorified in me. Don't let me do anything that will get in the way of that (Matthew 5:13–16).

Lord, I give myself to You. Help me to do my best to be a worker who needs not be ashamed of anything, someone who does a good job handling Your truth (2 Timothy 2:15). I refuse to let drugs get in Your way!

God, don't let sin reign in my flesh, in the form of drugs or anything else. I don't want to obey anything that has to do with sin. I don't want my body to be used for anything but Your righteousness. I give myself to You; in fact, I give You my entire body to use as Your instrument. I don't want sin to have any dominion over me, for I know that Your grace is mine (Romans 6:12–14).

Create in me a clean spirit, loving Lord, and renew in me a steadfast spirit (Psalm 51:10).

Dysfunctional Relationships

No one came with me. Everyone abandoned me. . . .
But the Lord stood with me and gave me strength.

2 TIMOTHY 4:16–17 NLT

It's hard to cope with relationships that are broken. We keep hoping that somehow things will change. That in spite of the way things have always gone in the past, *this time* things will be different.

We play our own role in these dysfunctional relationships. We may be what counselors call an enabler, allowing the individuals involved to keep on doing things that hurt. Or we may get sucked into the fights and the insults, the unproductive conversations and the hurtful habits.

But God wants to heal our entire lives, including our relationships. This healing is not likely to happen overnight—but our God can do amazing things. A miracle that takes time is still a miracle!

Creator God, I focus so often on how I want
others to change. I pray for them, I nag them,
I lecture them, I beg them, I try to manipulate
them. Ultimately, none of it does much good.
Instead, God, show me where *I* need to change.
I put myself into Your hands. I'm willing to have
You do whatever it takes to heal my relationships.

Create in me a clean spirit, loving Lord,
and renew in me a steadfast spirit
(Psalm 51:10).

Remind me, God, not to judge You by
the human relationships that have let me down.
Thank You that You are the perfect and
ever-loving Friend. You never seek to use me or
manipulate me. Instead, You constantly heal me
and help me become more truly free of all that
holds me back. Your love will never fail me.

Dear Father, I feel selfish and guilty taking
time for myself. I long to run away—but I'm
afraid of what I'll find when I come back.
Remind me that I'm no use to anyone if I don't
take care of myself. Give me the courage to set
boundaries that protect my own well-being.

When I am hurt, Lord, by these broken
relationships in my life, remind me to cling to
You. Truly, You alone are all I need. In You,
I am safe. In You, I am loved. In You,
I can enjoy the life You give me,
no matter what those I love do or say.

Jesus, I need help. I can't cope with this
relationship on my own any longer. I need a
counselor, a friend, a support group—something!
Someone who will understand what I'm going
through, Someone who can give me advice.
Please help me find the right person, the person
who will reveal Your light and wisdom to me.

Elderly Parents

*Listen with respect to the father who raised you,
and when your mother grows old, don't neglect her.*

PROVERBS 23:22 MSG

The scripture makes clear that we owe a debt of love and responsibility to our parents as they grow older. It may not always be an easy debt to fill. After all, our lives are already busy, filled with responsibilities to family and home, career and community. Our parents' growing needs seldom come at a time that's convenient for us. Instead, the season of life when we're the busiest with our own families and lives, doing our best to juggle all of life's growing demands, is the very time when our parents are likely to need more of our time and attention.

We may be surprised, though, to find that as our parents age, our changed relationship with them has its rewards as well. Our parents are not too old to offer us love and advice, if we can open our hearts to them. God will bless us through them—sometimes in surprising ways!

Loving Lord, I pray that You will be with my parents. I know You were with them before I was ever born. You were there when they were babies, and You are with them now in their old age. You will continue to carry them. You made them, and You will always be with them (Isaiah 46:3–4).

God, use me to bless my parents.
And let me be open to Your blessing
coming to me through them.

Jesus, You—who came to us directly from the Father—were willing to serve us. You even washed Your disciples' feet. Make me able and willing to follow Your example now and serve my parents, in whatever ways they need me. Show me that even if I need to help them dress, bathe, or go to the bathroom, Your Spirit can be gloried—and I, too, will be blessed in new ways.

Heavenly Father, may my parents flourish like tall trees planted in Your house. May they still bear fruit, even in their old age. Give them spirits that are ever young and growing (Psalm 92:12–14).

God, give me ears to hear my parents' wisdom,
even when it lies hidden beneath dementia or
illness. May I honor them with love, as they have
honored me. Let me give back to them from the
wealth they gave me when I was young.
Fill their old age with joy and peace.

You know how busy I am, Lord. It's hard for me
to sort out the demands on my time. Show me
what my priorities should be. Give me wisdom
to know how to help my parents as they age.

Enemies

*"You're familiar with the old written law,
'Love your friend,' and its unwritten companion, 'Hate your
enemy.' I'm challenging that. I'm telling you to love your
enemies. Let them bring out the best in you, not the
worst. . . . Live generously and graciously toward others,
the way God lives toward you."*

MATTHEW 5:43–44, 48 MSG

Sometimes Christians ignore what Jesus says here in the Gospel of Matthew. We make enemies out of the people we don't approve of, the people who disagree with what we believe, who have different politics, different values, different agendas. We might deny that we treat them like enemies—but do we act as though we love them? Do we give them our best? Do we pray for them with all our energy?

Jesus tells us that we can't be His mature followers—in fact, we can't even realize our own God-given identities—if we don't start treating everyone, including our enemies, with the same grace and generosity God has shown us.

Dear Jesus, help me to follow Your example always. Let me not work to get even with those who have hurt me. Remind me that if I seek revenge, I am only multiplying the evil in this world. Instead, help me to love.

Lord, bless this person who hurt me so badly. Do good in his life. Be with the person who disagrees with me. Bring good things to her. I ask that Your love would shine in her life.

Holy Spirit, fill me with Your love. Help me to
not only love You but all those whom You have
created. Teach me not to be so sensitive to slights
and insults. Help me to focus always on what is
good for others, rather than myself.
Teach me to love as You love.

God, You know how angry I feel right now
with this person. Show me her perspective.
You know how hurt I am. Reveal to
me the ways I have hurt him.
You know I am filled with hate.
Turn my hate into Your love.

Lord, if I only treat well those I agree with, those who are kind to me, those who love me, then I'm not showing the world Your love. Help me to love those who disagree with me, those who are unkind, those who are filled with hate. Use me to spread peace and love throughout the world.

God, make me willing to open my heart to those people I don't like. Turn my enemies into friends. You have power to transform all relationships. Do what seems impossible. Bring harmony and friendship to my world.

Jesus, You treated Your enemies with love and respect. Help me to follow Your example. May I not be overcome by evil, but instead, by the power of Your Spirit, may I overcome evil with good (Romans 12:21).

Facing Death

*"Well done, my good and faithful servant. . . .
Let's celebrate together!"*

MATTHEW 25:21 NLT

We fear the unknown—and death is the greatest unknown there is. As Christians, we say we believe in the resurrection of the dead, but deep in our hearts, we wonder what that means. The closer death comes to us, the harder it may be for us to hold on to our confidence in eternal life. And when death starts breathing down our necks—as we grow older or if we face a terminal illness—we are forced to confront our doubts head-on. Is there really anything beyond death? Or will all that we are cease to exist once we stop breathing?

The Bible assures us that physical death is not the end. Jesus came to this earth so that our fears could be put to rest. He has promised us that He has prepared a place for us in the life to come—and when we die, we will hear His voice welcoming us into the eternal celebration.

God, I'm trying to accept what lies ahead.
But I have to tell You, death is no friend of mine!
This isn't what I want. It feels unnatural.
It feels wrong.
I'm glad that Your Son felt the same way about it.
He prayed for a way around death,
if there was any way possible. And I'm glad Your
scripture refers to death as the "last enemy."
I like knowing that You and I are in this together.
Death is *not* natural. It's not what You intended.
You created me to live forever.
And because of Jesus, I will.

Jesus, be with those I love and have to leave
behind. I trust them to Your care. I know You
will be with them even when I no longer can be.

Lord, I feel so lonely. I don't want to burden the people I love with my feelings. I know they're dealing with my approaching death in their own way. They can't help me with what I'm facing. I'm all alone. Thank You that You're here with me. I'm counting on You in a way I never have before.

Jesus, even though I'm walking through the valley of the shadow of death, I'm not afraid. I know You are with me. You protect and comfort me. You're setting the table for me, a place where I can sit down and be nourished, right here in death's presence. Your goodness and mercy follow me wherever I go, and I know I will live forever with You (Psalm 23:4–6).

All my life, I've been looking at a dim reflection of You in a poor mirror, Lord, catching cloudy glimpses of who You are. Pretty soon, though, I'm going to see You face to face, with perfect clarity. I'll know You completely, just as You know me
(1 Corinthians 13:12).

Jesus, when I read about Your death on the cross,
I can tell You went through much of what I'm
experiencing now. You felt lonely and forsaken.
You wondered where God was. You felt death's
pain and horror. And yet in the midst of
all that, You still trusted Your Father.
You put Your spirit in His hands.
God, I want to follow Your Son's example.
I commit my spirit into Your hands.

Jesus, You endured death because You had Your
eyes on the joy that lay ahead (Hebrews 12:2).
Give me a glimpse of that same joy. May it be my
focal point, even in the midst of pain and fear.

Failure

Can anything ever separate us from Christ's love?
Does it mean he no longer loves us if we have trouble
or calamity, or are persecuted, or hungry, or destitute,
or in danger, or threatened with death? . . .
No, despite all these things, overwhelming victory
is ours through Christ, who loved us.

ROMANS 8:35, 37 NLT

We all want to be successful. Countless books have been written on the topic, offering us yet another secret formula for guaranteeing that success will be ours. But the reality is this: we all experience failures.

Even the great heroes of our Christian faith experienced their share of failure. Abraham and Moses, Elijah and David, Peter and Paul—they all knew what it was like to make serious mistakes. But God used even their failures to bring them to the place where He wanted them to be.

And He will do the same for us. No matter how many times we fail, His love never does. And in the midst of our failures, we can still find victory in Christ.

Loving Lord, You know I long to be a success.
I want to live the victorious Christian life.
I want to please You. I want others to be
impressed with my faith. I want to be the person
You created. I know my motives are all mixed
up—but I do sincerely want to follow You.
And yet again and again, I fail. I let You down.
I let others down. I let myself down.
Teach me, Lord, to find You even in the
midst of failure. Let me never put off holding
out my arms to You, so that You can pick me up
and put me back on my feet. Thank You
that Your grace never fails.

Sometimes, Jesus, I feel so afraid of failure that I can't seem to do anything at all. I don't even want to try something in case I won't be successful. My fear paralyzes me. Christ Jesus, release me from my fear, I pray. Remind me not to take myself so seriously. Help me to see that the world won't end if I fail. Give me joy in the effort, whatever the results.

Even though my efforts often fail, Lord, help me to remember that *I* am never a failure. My worth is safe, for it comes from You.

God, Abraham failed You when he fled to Egypt during the drought. Moses lost his temper and turned to violence more than once. David committed both adultery and murder. Peter denied Your Son. And yet You used all the people who failed You so badly. Use me, too.

Help me to learn from my failures, loving Lord.
Use them to help me grow.

Remind me, Jesus, that sometimes what
the world considers failure is not failure at
all from eternity's perspective. After all, Your
disciples must have assumed at first that Your
death on the cross was the worst failure of all.
And yet what looked like failure brought
new life to all Creation.

Family Feuds

*"The Sun of Righteousness will rise with healing
in his wings. And you will go free."*

MALACHI 4:2 NLT

Do you dread family get-togethers? Are holidays
occasions for conflict? Do long-standing family feuds
mar what should be happy family times?

We're not talking about fights between *different*
families; we're talking about intrafamily feuds, the kind
between aunts and uncles, between sisters and brothers,
or between grandparents and parents. Maybe they lurk
beneath the surface, bursting out unexpectedly over some
small issue. Or maybe they're expressed in icy silence
that's never broken. Maybe you wish everyone would just
grow up. Or maybe you're a part of the feud.

God longs to bring His love to your family's life. His
Spirit is waiting to seep into the cracks in the anger, to
water the hurt feelings with healing, to slowly bring new
life to what has been broken so long. Will you open your
own heart to let the process begin? God longs to heal you
and set you free.

Dear Father, the whole world is crying out for peace—peace between nations and even peace within homes. We long for peace in our family as well, the kind of peace that comes from walking in step with each other and with You. Help us to learn the laws of peace and how to foster harmony in our family through Your Word.

Bring peace to my family, Lord. Heal our ancient wounds. Build bridges between us. May we find the way to love each other again.

God, when I read the Old Testament, I realize
You know all about flawed families. Jacob and
Esau plotted for their father's favor. Joseph's
brothers sold him into slavery. David's own son
conspired to murder him. And yet You used these
broken families. Countless generations have
learned of You from their stories, and from
their genetic line, Your Son was born.
Father, I pray that You would use my family,
too, despite its flaws. Shed Your grace over us.
Transform us.

Jesus, how can I love these people who have hurt me so deeply? I don't even want to see their faces, let alone forgive them. And yet You ask me to love my enemies, to bless those who curse me. Give me the strength and courage to obey You.

Lord, be more than important to me than anyone. May I find my worth only in You. When You are everything to me, then my family's actions will no longer matter so much. And when I no longer need their love and acceptance to know my own worth, I can finally be free to forgive them.

Family Stress

O thou afflicted, tossed with tempest, and not comforted, behold, I will set thy stones in fair colors, and lay thy foundations with sapphires.

ISAIAH 54:11 ASV

Family life is full of stress. Relationships, conflicting responsibilities, busy schedules—all of them contribute to the tension that often escalates within our homes. When something out of the ordinary comes along—a death in the family, a fire, a job loss, a serious illness—the stress can mount to nearly unbearable levels.

And yet stress can also be what makes our families strong. When we find ways to meet the challenges together, we draw closer to one another. When we weather another crisis, we can thank God that He has guided our family through the storm. He is building a strong and beautiful foundation for our family's future.

Lord, may even our chores tie us together
in a new way. Give us joy and laughter as we
wash the dishes or do the laundry, take out the
garbage or mop the kitchen floor. May we
learn to enjoy our time together.

With all our busy schedules, God, You know
how hard it is to ever find time to sit down
together. Help us to make time to share a meal
together at least once each day. Draw us together
around the table. As we share food, may
we also share each other's lives.

You know how stressed our family is, Father.
Remind us to set aside time now and then from
the rush and hurry, time to simply relax together.
Give us common interests that tie us together.
Make us open to exploring new activities
together. Bless us, I pray, and make our
family life more fun!

When we're always in such a hurry, God, it's hard to have the energy to address the problems that come up in our family's life. May we never be in too much of a hurry to share our hearts and listen to each other. Help us together to find the solutions to our family's problems.

Loving Father, You know that sometimes the "adult problems" in our family seem to overshadow the children's. Remind us, Lord, that the death of a goldfish or a cross word from a teacher can be as stressful to our family's younger members as professional challenges and financial worries are to the older ones.

Jesus, help us not to blame each other for the stress we face. Instead, may we work together and help one another.

Give us the insight to see which parts of
our family's situation can be changed, God.
Reveal to us the unhealthy habits that keep us
constantly stressed—and give us the courage and
determination to break those habits together.
Strengthen us to rise above the circumstances
that can't be changed and find ways
to live with them creatively.

Lord, help our family to pray the serenity prayer:
"Grant us the serenity to accept the things we
cannot change, the courage to change the things
we can, and the wisdom to know the difference."

Fear

God is our refuge and strength,
an ever-present help in trouble.
Therefore we will not fear,
though the earth give way and the mountains
fall into the heart of the sea.

PSALM 46:1–2 NIV

Fear is a normal and healthy biological reaction that alerts us to danger. Unfortunately, in our lives, fear and danger no longer necessarily go together. Instead, fear can exist all on its own. When that happens, fear becomes destructive and crippling. As Franklin D. Roosevelt said, "The only thing we have to fear is fear itself."

When we find ourselves in bondage to fear, God holds the key that can set us free. When life seems threatening, filled with unknown (and possibly imaginary) dangers, He will be our refuge. He is always there. In Him, we can always be secure.

Lord, You are my light and my salvation. Whom shall I fear? You are the strength of my life. Of whom shall I be afraid? When my emotional enemies attack me, they'll stumble and fall. Though an entire army of fears come against me, my heart will be strong. Even in the midst of a war, I can be confident in You, because I ask You for only one thing: that I may dwell in Your house all the days of my life, seeing Your beauty. For I know that in the time of trouble, You will hide me in Your pavilion. You'll tuck me away in a secret nook inside Your tabernacle; You'll set me on a rock where I'll be safe, where I can lift up my head and see over the heads of my enemies. And that's why, Lord, I sing to You with joy (Psalm 27:1–6)!

Thank You, Jesus, that You have given me Your peace. I know Your peace is not like anything the world has to offer me. Because of You, I will not let my heart be troubled, neither will I let it be afraid (John 14:27).

For You, Lord, have not given me a spirit of bondage to fear. Instead, Your Spirit has adopted me. And now, whenever I am scared, I can cry, "Daddy! Father!" (Romans 8:15).

Since You are my light and salvation, Lord,
what should I be afraid of? You are my
stronghold—so why should I
fear anything (Psalm 27:1)?

You are with me, Lord, so I won't be afraid.
What can human beings do to me
when I have You (Psalm 118:6)?

You didn't give me a timid spirit, God,
but a spirit of power, of love, and
of self-discipline (2 Timothy 1:7).

Financial Strain

My God shall supply every need of yours according to his riches in glory in Christ Jesus.

<small>PHILIPPIANS 4:19 ASV</small>

God uses our financial needs to draw us closer to Him. He hasn't promised that we will be rich, nor does He demand that we be penniless. Instead, He wants us to simply trust Him, whatever our finances. Even in the midst of financial stress, He offers us the prosperity and abundance of His grace. He has promised to meet our every need.

Lord, why am I anxious about having enough money for the clothes I need? Remind me that the flowers of the field don't work or do anything at all, and yet You clothe them gloriously. If You clothe the grass, which is alive for such a fleeting time, remind me that You will certainly clothe me! Help me not be anxious about my finances. When I say, "What are we going to eat?" or "How will I buy what we need to drink?" or "Will we have enough money for clothes?" reassure me that You already know I need these things. Give me the strength to seek Your Kingdom before anything else—and leave my finances in Your hands (Matthew 6:28–33).

Dear Jesus, help me to follow Your commands. Even when I am financially stressed, may I give to others, knowing that You will give back to me—good measure, pressed down, shaken together, and running over. You have enough for me—but you will use the same measure to meet my needs that I use to give to others (Luke 6:38).

Let me not sow sparingly, God. Instead, show me how to scatter seeds everywhere so that I can also reap bountifully. Let me give to others willingly, cheerfully, without grudging. No matter what my finances, I know Your grace will be enough. You will give me all I need to give to others (2 Corinthians 9:6–8).

Teach me, Jesus, to be content in whatever
financial situation I find myself. Teach me how
to have next to nothing—and how to have
more than enough. In any and every financial
circumstance, teach me the secret of facing either
plenty or hunger, abundance or need. I believe
You will supply my every need from Your riches
in glory (Philippians 4:11–13, 19).

God, thank You that I can be confident that I can
ask You for anything, knowing that You hear me.
Since You hear me, You will answer me
(1 John 5:14). I give you my finances, Father.
I bring all my concerns to You. I trust
You to take care of everything.

Foreclosure

*Jesus replied, "Foxes have dens and birds have nests,
but the Son of Man has no place to lay his head."*

LUKE 9:58 NIV

Our homes are important parts of our identity.
They give us security and comfort. When we lose
them, we feel adrift and frightened. The loss is
greater than just a financial problem; it strikes at
our very hearts. It doesn't seem possible that we
can be forced to give up something so intimately
our own. Even birds have nests, and even foxes
have holes in the ground they think of as home!

Jesus knew what it was like to be without a
home. Once He was an adult, He had no home
of His own. He understands how people feel who
are forced to give up their houses. He walks with
them through this time. And He holds out His
arms, longing to offer them the shelter of His love.

Lord, make me a good listener for those who are going through the pain of foreclosure. Let me not judge or be impatient. Give me the wisdom to give good advice. Make me willing to be useful in any way I can be, even if it includes opening my own home.

God, our economy is so complicated. Remind us that our own mistakes are mixed up with those of many others. We cannot untangle what is already done. Help us focus instead on the future. May we learn from the past as we move forward. Give us wisdom to plan carefully for whatever comes next.

I'm so confused, Lord. There are so many legal and financial things to be done. Show me where to seek the knowledge I need to find my way.

Remind us, Father, that our family is more than a house. Give us places to be together and feel safe. Be with each one of us, especially the youngest members of our family, as we struggle to make our way through this difficult time.

Be our Home now, Creator God.
May we realize in a new way that
You are all we truly need to feel safe.

I am grieving the loss of our house, Jesus.
Remind me that it's okay to go through all the
stages of grief, and that You will walk with me
through each one. As I scream, "This can't be
happening to me!" You are there. When I rage
against the world, You wait patiently beside me.
When I seek to bargain with You, promising You
I'll be a better person if You'll only let me keep
my house, Your patience never falters. When I
sink into depression, Your arms reach out to me.
And one day, You will lift me up into acceptance.
Only then, will I be ready for whatever
You have in store next for me.

Greed

Then he said, "Beware!
Guard against every kind of greed.
Life is not measured by how much you own."

LUKE 12:15 NLT

We've often heard it said that money is the root of all evil. Actually, however, the Bible says that *the love of money* is the root of evil (1 Timothy 6:10). In other words, it's greed that gets us in trouble. Money itself is merely a useful tool that can be used for either good or bad.

But greed is the urge to get more and more of something, whether it be money or food or possessions. The greedy person is too attached to the things of this world. And as a result, the greedy person is often anxious, worried about losing what he already has.

The generous person, however, is truly free. She can open her hands and take the good things God brings into her life. And she can just as easily open her hands and let them go. It gives her joy to share, and loss doesn't worry her. She knows that God has plenty to give her, and His grace will never be exhausted.

Dearest Lord, remind me that when I am greedy and acquisitive, someone else often pays the price. My abundance may deprive others of what they truly need. Make me willing to get by with less so that others will have enough. Teach me to share.

Jesus, reveal to me my greed. Help me recognize my true priorities. Make me see where I spend too much. Show me things I could do without. Help me resist the persistent voices that come at me constantly in commercials and ads, telling me I need *more*. Create in me a generous heart.

What good are riches, Lord, if I don't use them to help others?

Show me, God, that greed weighs me down.
It doesn't give me joy. Instead, when greed rules
my heart, I am never satisfied. Nothing is ever
enough. I can't enjoy what I have, because
I'm too focused on what I *don't* have.

Give me pleasure, heavenly Father, in the things
that are truly most important, the things that
cannot be accumulated. . .like a child's laugh,
a friend's presence, or a beautiful sunset.

Remind me, Lord, that my value does not depend on what I own. Instead, may I see that greed comes between You and me, between others and me, and even between me and my true self.

Help me, Christ Jesus, to put to death within me all that leads me away from You. Destroy my greed, for when I am greedy, I am worshipping false gods. Let me only worship You (Colossians 3:5).

Helplessness

*"But the tax collector stood at a distance. He would
not even look up to heaven, but beat his breast and said,
'God, have mercy on me, a sinner.' "*

LUKE 18:13 NIV

We've all heard the expression, "God helps those who help
themselves." And while there's a certain truth to the saying
(God doesn't want us to sit there expecting a miracle when
He's already put the means to accomplish something into
our hands), the opposite is also true: God helps those who
are helpless.

Look at the tax collector who didn't even try to
prove his worth. He just stood off at a distance and threw
himself on God's mercy. Alcoholics Anonymous teaches
that only when a person has hit bottom and finally
acknowledged her helplessness is she ready to change.

In Jesus' day, the Pharisees didn't see themselves as
helpless. They trusted in their own righteousness, in their
own abilities to save themselves. But Jesus said, "Blessed
are the poor in spirit, for theirs is the kingdom of heaven"
(Matthew 5:3 NIV). When we are helpless, when we give
up our dependence on our own strength, then God can
begin to act in our lives.

Lord, help me know the difference between
accepting that I need Your help—and using
a false helplessness to manipulate others.
Show me all You have already given me,
and give me the insight to use it.

Sometimes, Lord Jesus, when I feel helpless,
I'm really just underestimating the abilities You've
given me. Give me the strength and confidence
to become the person You created me to be.

I need You, God. I can't handle life on my own.

Lord, You promise to give me all that I need.
I depend on You for my help.

Sometimes, Father, I feel helpless
to change the way others perceive me.
Thank You that You always believe in me.

God, give me a healthy humility that depends
on Your strength as my help and refuge.
May my sense of helplessness not be based
on lies I tell myself, however. When I hear myself
saying things like, "There's no way I can get out
of this mess—it's hopeless," or "Life hasn't been
fair to me, so I why should I even try anymore?"
or "No one cares about me so I might as well
give up," remind me that these words are not the
truth. Give me the courage that's based
on confidence in Your strength.

Hidden Sin

*"People look at the outward appearance,
but the Lord looks at the heart."*

1 Samuel 16:7 niv

If sin is anything that comes between God and us,
then we are simply deceiving ourselves if we think
there's any point in burying our sins out of sight
where no one can see it. Sin that is hidden still
gets in the way of our relationship with God. By
hiding it out of sight, we may think we have fooled
other people. We may even fool ourselves. We do
not fool God.

In the New Testament, Jesus makes clear
that our hidden thoughts are just as serious and
damaging as our external behaviors. He wants us
to be people of integrity and wholeness, without
any darkness festering inside us. He knows that
ultimately, it is our own selves that are hurt most by
these shameful secrets.

Lord, Your Word tells me that You will
one day judge the secrets of every heart
(Romans 2:16). You will bring everything to
judgment, everything that is hidden,
whether good or evil (Ecclesiastes 12:14).
In the Gospels, You said that everything that
is covered up will be revealed, and everything
that's hidden will be known. The things I thought
I said when I was all alone will be proclaimed
from the housetops (Luke 12:2–3). How
embarrassing! Give me the courage, Lord, to
bring my sin into the light of Your Spirit.

God, this hidden sin eats away at my heart.
I have no peace because of it.
Help me to give it to You.

Jesus, show me the sins I hide even from myself.
Reveal to me the unhealthy thought habits
I cling to. Remind me that if I nurse my
hatred toward another, then I am guilty
of spiritual murder. And if I allow lustful
thoughts to become an obsession, then I am
committing the essence of adultery.

Teach me, Lord, to never be dishonest with
myself or You. Examine my heart, and reveal its
contents. May there be no secrets between us.

I realize, Lord, that when I act as though I'm a good and righteous person, all the while hiding my sins out of sight, then I'm also guilty of hypocrisy. Hypocrisy lies around my heart like a wall, keeping others out, keeping You out.

Jesus, You called hypocrisy the "leaven of the Pharisees" (Luke 12:1 asv). It's something that ferments inside me. It grows, doubles, fills me up, the way yeast does. Remove it from me, I pray. Clean out my heart.

God, I gaze into the mirror of Your Word. Reveal to me anything that comes between us.

Hopelessness

"For I know the plans I have for you," declares the
LORD, *"plans to prosper you and not to harm you,*
plans to give you hope and a future."

JEREMIAH 29:11 NIV

We tend to think of hope as a cheery, optimistic
outlook on life. But the biblical concept of hope
is far greater and deeper. It is a confidence and
expectation in what God will do in the future, an
understanding that the same God who was with
us yesterday will be with us tomorrow.

When things seem hopeless, we are robbed of
this confidence. We feel as though the future is
empty and barren. But hopelessness is always a lie,
for our God has big plans for us! No matter how
hard the road, it always leads us into His presence.

Why do I get so depressed, Lord?
Why do I surrender my peace?
Help me to hope in You, knowing that
soon I will be praising You for all You have done.
You are the one who will make me smile again.
You are my God (Psalm 43:5).

Lord, I put my hope in You,
for Your love never fails (Psalm 130:7).

Thank You, God, that You have plans
for me—plans to bless me and prosper me.
I know that Your plans are often not the same as
mine. But You know what the future holds,
and I trust You.

Jesus, You promised to never leave me
or forsake me. Because of You, I have hope.
I know this hope will never be put to shame.

I called to You, Lord, out of my distress—
and You answered me! When I was drowning,
surrounded by an ocean of despair, with waves
billowing over my head, I was sure that You were
no longer paying attention to my life. I felt as
though I was about to be destroyed. I was sure
my life was over. But You brought me up from
the pit of despair, Lord. You heard my prayer,
even when I felt as though I was spiritually
fainting. Lord, help me not to put my trust in
anything or anyone but You. When I do, I forsake
my hope in Your steadfast love. My salvation
comes from You (Jonah 2:2–7)!

Infertility

*Hannah was in deep anguish, crying bitterly as
she prayed to the LORD. And she made this vow:
"O LORD of Heaven's Armies, if you will look upon my
sorrow and answer my prayer and give me a son, then I
will give him back to you."*

1 SAMUEL 1:10, 11 NLT

When you can't become pregnant, it suddenly seems as
though every woman you see is expecting. Everywhere
you turn, there are reminders that you cannot achieve
this thing you long for. From diaper commercials to
the unthinking questions of people wondering when
you're going to start your family, you feel bombarded
by your lack. You may feel as though you are unworthy,
worthless.

God wants you to see this as a lie. The longing for
a child is a perfectly natural one. But when we become
obsessed with wanting anything—no matter how good
it might be—we turn it into a god. Our value does not
depend on our ability to do anything. It comes from
God—and we can trust Him to fulfill the deepest
longings of our hearts in the way that is best for us.

Lord, I'm trying to accept whatever
You want for my life. But it's so hard.
You know how much I long for a child.
Help me to give this longing to You.

God, I know You can work miracles. Work in me.
Work in my body. I surrender myself to You.

Help my husband, Lord, as well.
May our longing for a child not drive us apart. Give
us patience with each other's different perspectives.
Whether or not we ever have a child, may our
marriage always be fruitful.

I'm seeking You, Lord. You promised that You would answer me and deliver me from all my fears. You know how much I fear that I will never be a mother, and so, in the face of my fear, I claim that promise as my own. I praise You that You are with me, that I have no need to feel discouraged or worried about any fertility issues that may lay ahead. Thank you that You are my strength and my help. Bring peace to my troubled heart as You uphold me with Your righteous right hand (Psalm 34:4; Isaiah 41:10; John 14:27).

I feel so angry and frustrated that I can't become pregnant, God. Please calm my heart with Your love, for Your love is patient and kind, and not easily angered. Help me to be slow in my speech and slow in anger when it comes to dealing with my spouse, my family members, friends, or my doctor. Transform my anger into something creative, Lord, something that can be used for Your glory.

God, I am struggling with envy and jealousy as I see pregnant women and hear of new babies in others' lives. Teach me not to compare my life with others. Free me from the bitterness that lives inside me, so that I can rejoice in the new life You send into the world.

Each month, Lord, I am filled with hope again— and then each month, my hopes are dashed again. I am tired of hoping. I don't know how to keep going. Lead me, loving Lord. Make the way ahead clear to me.

Heavenly Father, You put this desire to be a mother into my heart. You have promised to give me the desires of my heart—and so I trust this desire to You. I believe that even if You don't satisfy my desires in the way I hope, You will never forget or overlook any heart's desire. I will delight myself in You, trusting in Your love (Psalm 37:4).

Injustice

Do what is fair and just to your neighbor.

Micah 6:8 msg

Did you know that in the Gospels, Jesus talks more about justice for those who are poor than He does about violence or sexual immorality? In fact, about a tenth of all the verses in the four Gospels have to do with concern for the poor.

We live in a world of injustice. A third of all the children in the world's developing nations suffer from malnutrition. Almost three million children die each year from hunger. This isn't fair. And God cares.

He wants us to care, too. He doesn't want us to look away from the world's injustice. He wants us to face it—and fight it.

Lord, You say to me, "Do justice and
righteousness, and deliver from the hand
of the oppressor those who have been robbed
of their rights. Do no harm to those who are
aliens and strangers. Don't hurt the children
and women who live in single-parent families"
(Jeremiah 22:3, 4). Give me the courage and the
faith to fight injustice wherever I see it.

When the world seems so unjust to me, Lord,
remind me that it treated You the same way.
Shift my focus away from myself.
Show me ways to help others whose
situation is far worse than mine.

God, you call me to share what I have with
those who have less than me (Proverbs 22:16).
You ask me to be kind to strangers, to those
who are aliens in our land (Exodus 22:21).
You remind me to treat with respect those
who have apparently lower positions
than I do (Job 31:13–14).

Father, teach me to practice justice in even the
smallest areas of my life. Reveal to me the truth
of my actions. Help me see that the choices
I make affect the lives of others.

Lord, when the world treats me unfairly,
remind me of what You endured.

Give me Your attitude, Jesus.
May I think less about what I deserve,
and more about the other person.
Show me how to turn the other cheek
when I am injured (Matthew 5:39).
Help me to always follow Your example.
Remind me that vengeance is never justice.

Insomnia

He grants sleep to those he loves.

PSALM 127:2 NIV

Insomnia can be a terrible issue. It makes us tired and cranky. When we're tired, we're more likely to feel anxious or depressed, more easily angered, less patient. It becomes a vicious circle: the more upset and tense we become, the less we can sleep; the less we sleep, the more upset and tense we become. . . .

We may end up afraid to even go to bed because we don't want to face the frustration we feel when we lie there awake again. Anxiety overwhelms us and we feel helpless.

But God is with us, even when we lie awake night after night. He has compassion on our sleeplessness. His love never fails.

Father, tonight I give my insomnia to You.
If I stay awake all night, then that's okay.
I'll be comfortable here in my bed, resting in
Your presence. I submit my thoughts to You.
I dwell in Your peace, and I take refuge
in Your presence. Help me to be like the
apostle Paul, able to be content in whatever
circumstances—including sleeplessness!

Dear God, You know how my insomnia makes me suffer. I have prayed for Your help and healing—but You haven't seemed to answer. Teach my spirit to be still in the quiet moments of the night when I cannot sleep. Remind me to use this time for prayer.

Loving Father, fill my heart with peace tonight. May I relax in Your presence.

Dearest God, as I lie here in bed, may I feel the echo of Your Spirit's breath in my own breathing. May the peace of Your presence lie over me like a blanket. May I recall all the things You have done for me over the years. Help me rest.

Lord, take away the worries that plague me when I lie awake. As each new anxiety rises to the surface of my thoughts, help me turn it over to You.

Job Loss

Wealth from hard work grows over time.

Proverbs 13:11 nlt

Losing a job is a painful experience. We look to our jobs for status and security. Without them, our identities may seem less certain, less valuable even. We are filled with anxiety for the future. Now that this calamity has come upon us, we worry that even worse things lie ahead. How will we be able to pay our bills? Will we lose our house? What if we end up homeless and on the street?

But God is with us in these circumstances, just as He always is. He asks us to be patient. He assures us that if we are willing to work hard, we will have financial security once more. And He promises He is still working in our lives.

Lord, You know this time of unemployment
is not what I had hoped for. But let me use it
nevertheless to grow and rest and be useful to
others. Help me to use this time wisely.

Give me wisdom to manage my finances, Father.
Show me how to adjust my lifestyle to these
new circumstances. Remind me that all
I truly need to be happy is Your presence.

Lead me to a new job, I pray, dear Lord. Show
me where to look. I thank You for the new people
and new opportunities that lie ahead.

I don't know where to turn for help, Jesus.
Show me people who are willing and able
to guide me. Teach me how to network!

Do I have any skills I've been overlooking, Lord?
Is there something new You want me
to be open to doing? Make this
an opportunity for me to grow.

Father, thank You that You have a plan for me.
Even when I can't see what it is,
lead me one step at a time.

Take my hands, God, and use them for
whatever work You want me to do.
Take my feet, God, and lead me to the job
openings where You want me to apply.
Take my voice, God, and during each job
interview, give me the words You want me to say.
Take my eyes, God, and teach them to search for
the job opportunities You want me to see.
Take my mind, God, and give me the
new ideas You want me to consider.
Take my soul, God, and fill me with Your Spirit
in a new way during this time of unemployment.
Take my life, God, and whether I have
a job or am unemployed, use me for
the purposes of Your heart.

Job Stress

Work willingly at whatever you do, as though you were working for the Lord rather than for people.

COLOSSIANS 3:23 NLT

Our jobs are often the source of much of the stress in our lives. Tight deadlines, multiple responsibilities, conflicts with coworkers and supervisors—all these can lead to tension. We're likely to spend about half our lives in our workplaces, though, so we need to find joy and satisfaction, rather than stress and anxiety, in our jobs.

We can learn to sense God's presence with us as we work. Even on our busiest days, we need to take time to whisper a prayer or spend a quiet moment with our Lord.

God, lead me today. May I serve You as I work.
Thank You for the opportunity to do this job.
May I do it for You, as a labor of love.

Lord Jesus, as I enter this workplace,
I bring Your presence with me.
May I speak Your peace and grace to everyone
with whom I interact today. I acknowledge Your
lordship over all that will be said and done today.

Be with each of my interactions today.
May others see You in me.

Thank You, loving Lord, for the gifts You have given me. Help me to use them responsibly and well today as I do my work. Anoint my creativity, my ideas, and my energy, so that even the smallest tasks will bring Your light to the world.

Heavenly Lord, thank You for my job. May I be
challenged and inspired by the work I do. Even
in the midst of stress, even on the days when I
fail, may I look away from my own feelings and
see You—and beyond You, a world that needs my
efforts, no matter how small they may seem.
Give me the will and strength to work hard
today. May I find gladness in my efforts,
and most of all, may I please You.

Father, when I am confused at work, guide me.
When I am weary, energize me.
When I am burned out, shine the light
of Your Holy Spirit on me.

Litigation

And thou shalt speak unto him, and put the words in his mouth: and I will be with thy mouth, and with his mouth, and will teach you what ye shall do.

EXODUS 4:15 ASV

Bringing lawsuits against each other has become commonplace in our world today. This is not necessarily a bad thing. It is certainly better to turn to the courts to settle a problem rather than to use violence. We don't want to go back to the days of the Wild West, where the fastest gun ruled! It's unfortunate, however, that so many of today's conflicts are unable to be settled by people simply working out a compromise.

When litigation is filed against us, it's a stressful situation. We will feel afraid and angry. It is hard to know the right course of action to take.

But God will be with us! He will be give us the words to say—and He will also be with the other side, the person who is taking us to court. His Holy Spirit doesn't take sides, and He always works for peace.

Lord, as I face this legal battle, I clothe myself
with Your righteousness, integrity, and love.
Thank You that You are always present with me.
Help me to be honest, both with myself and
with those who are taking me to court.
Show me if I am at fault. Free me from anger,
hate, and the desire for revenge.

Lord Jesus, I ask You that truth would prevail.
Protect me from those who tell lies about me.
Reassure me that You are my defense. May Your
Spirit give me the right words to speak.

Father, even now, make me willing and ready to
forgive (as You have forgiven me). Show us if
there is another option for settling this conflict.

Jesus, You told us to come to terms quickly with
our accusers on our way to court (Matthew 5:25).
I pray that You would open the door
to peace in this situation.

Lead me to the right legal counsel,
heavenly Father. May my attorney give me
advice that comes from You.

Loving God, You promise that You do
not hate me when others accuse me.
You will not hide Your face from me.
You will hear my cries (Psalm 22:24).

Help me, Lord! You know how scared I am
about this court case. Your Word tells me
that You are just and You are my defense.
Let me rely on You. Plead my cause.
Deliver me from this crisis. Be my rock of refuge,
my strong fortress in the midst of all this. Go
before me and fight this battle on my behalf.

Prodigal Children

All your children will be taught by the LORD,
and great will be their peace.

ISAIAH 54:13 NIV

There are few things that hurt quite so much as children who go astray. We long to run after them and bring them home—and yet we must respect their decisions. We ache to care for them and protect them the way we did when they were small—but they have gone beyond our protection. We feel so helpless.

But even when our children were babies, they were never truly ours. They always belonged to God. His hands held them. Only He kept them safe. And none of that has changed. Even now, if we have to sit back and watch as our children seem to run headlong toward danger, we can trust them to God's love. He is teaching them. He is shielding them. In the midst of what looks to us like chaos and confusion, He is there, leading our children into His peace.

My heart feels broken, Father. I know You
understand, for You, too, must be heartsick when
You watch Your children choose paths that lead
them toward brokenness and sorrow. Heal my
children, I pray, Lord. Lead them in Your paths.
I gave them to You when they were small—
and now I give them to You again.

How am I to blame, Lord? I search the past for
the answers. I agonize over my many mistakes.
I long to go back and redo portions of my life.
I am so sorry for the times I failed my children!
But Father, I know that only You are perfect.
Work in my children's lives, despite my failures.
Use even my mistakes to bring
them closer to You.

Jesus, in the story You told about the prodigal son, the father had the love and courage to let his child go. I ask that You give me the strength to do the same. Remind me not to lecture or nag. May I not judge. Give me grace to keep my mouth shut—and my heart open.

I feel so helpless to do anything to help my child, Lord. Remind me that prayer is never the least I can do. It is always the *most*. May I never grow tired of praying for my child.

God, I affirm that You know best what my children need. I let my children go. The way they have chosen seems wrong to me. But that's between them and You. I will trust Your Holy Spirit to work in their lives and hearts, leading them into truth. No matter how many times I forget, remind me once again to step back and give You room to work!

Father, give me patience to wait. I want my children's situation to be different *now*! I long for things to "get back to normal." I know I sometimes pressure my children to move faster in the direction I wish they would go. Help me trust Your timing in their lives.

Sickness

The LORD sustains them on their sickbed and restores them from their bed of illness.

PSALM 41:3 NIV

No one enjoys being sick! But at one time or another, it's an experience all of us have. When sickness forces us to step back from life, to retreat to the small world of our beds, God is with us there. He will sustain us and restore us. He may even have something He wants to teach us during this time of illness!

Father, I have so much to do.
How can I take time out to be sick?
I need Your healing hand, Lord. Renew my
strength—physically, emotionally, and spiritually.

Jesus, in the Gospels, You healed everyone who
asked for Your help. I'm asking now:
please make me better!

Be with me, Lord, here in this quiet room.
Let me not feel too sick to hear what
You have to say to me.

Dearest Lord, heal this one I love who is sick today. You have promised to redeem our lives from destruction, and I pray now that You will crown this person with your loving-kindness and tender mercies (Psalm 103:4). Thank You that You always hear our prayers.

God, I know that all circumstances can lead us to You, even sickness. I pray that You would use this time of pain and illness to Your greater glory.

Lord, I bless You with all my soul.
I will never forget all You have done for me.
You have forgiven me, You have redeemed me,
and You will heal me (Psalm 103:2–3).

Jesus, I'm sick again! I feel so frustrated
with my own body. Lord, is there something
You're trying to say to me? Help me examine my
life during this time while I'm in bed.
Is my lifestyle making me sick? Is there
something You want me to change?

Surgery

"Don't panic. I'm with you. There's no need to fear
for I'm your God. . . . I'll hold you steady,
keep a firm grip on you."

ISAIAH 41:10 MSG

As we face a surgery, our hearts are often filled
with fear. This procedure forces us to acknowledge
we cannot control our lives. We must surrender to
our doctors, trusting the outcome to them. . .and
to God. We go under anesthesia, uncertain what
we will find when we wake up. It seems a little like
death, a venture into a dark and unknown place!

But God's hands are sure. He holds us safe.
He will never let us drop, neither in this life nor in
the one to come.

Lord, I place my body in Your hands today.
Guide the medical professionals who will work
on my body. Give them skill and wisdom, sure
hands and alert minds. Use them to restore me
to health that You may be glorified.

Give me the courage, Jesus, to say the words
You spoke on the cross: Into Your hands
I commit my spirit.

God of power and might, guide my surgeon's
hands, I pray. May my body respond
quickly to this treatment. May I be
healed to serve You anew.

Jesus, my best Friend, You know how scared I
am as I face this surgery. What if something goes
wrong? What if there are complications? Will I
ever feel like myself again? How much pain will
I have to face during the recovery process?
In the midst of all these fears, Lord,
I cling to You. Yes, I'm terrified—
but nevertheless I trust You.

Lord, You are the Author of Life, the Great
Healer. You know all that is wrong inside
my body. Please be with me during this surgery.
Breathe Your peace into my heart.
Be with my family as they wait.
Assure them that You are in control.

Jesus, may the doctors and nurses who care for
me today sense Your presence in me.
Bless them through me, I pray.

Toxic Friendships

*Then Jonathan and David made a covenant,
because he loved him as his own soul.*

1 SAMUEL 18:3 ASV

The friendship between Jonathan and David was a healthy one. It fulfilled the Golden Rule, for each treated the other as he would choose to be treated himself.

Friendships become toxic, however, when they no longer have this quality of healthy love. Instead, the relationship becomes destructive. One side uses and manipulates the other. We may not realize how unhealthy and poisonous a relationship has become until the problem is bigger than we know how to handle. Even once we recognize the problem, we may not know what to do.

God never wants us to be involved in something that isn't healthy for us. When we find ourselves involved in a toxic friendship, we need to ask Him to show us the way to freedom—for our sake, for the sake of our friend, and for His sake as well. He is not glorified by a relationship that damages and destroys!

Lord, give me wisdom to recognize when a friendship is no longer healthy. I know that true friends support one another. They help each other overcome adversity. They help each other feel good about themselves. They accept one another unconditionally. They reflect Your love to each other. When I find myself involved with a relationship that doesn't have these qualities, give me the courage to make a change.

Jesus, I realize that after I've been with this friend, I often feel less sure of myself. I feel ashamed, embarrassed, less confident. That can't be what You want! Remind me to rely on Your love for my self-worth. Don't let me hand my identity over to this toxic relationship.

Lord, he did it again. He broke his promises to me. He let me down. I feel like such an idiot. Show me what to do now. Should I confront him? Should I let him know I can't trust him again? What would You do in my place? Please give me Your wisdom.

I found out that my friend has been gossiping about me, God. She's been talking about me behind my back. She's been sharing my confidences with people without my permission. How could she betray my trust like that? Lord Jesus, I know I've let You down in so many ways. Help me not to be self-righteous. Help me to forgive—but at the same time, help me to learn not to share my heart so openly with someone who has proven she can't be trusted.

God, I feel so lonely. I've spent an entire day
with my friend, but all I've done is listen to her
talk about her life. I don't want to be selfish,
Lord—but I had a problem I wanted to share
with someone, and she refused to listen.
I felt like all she wanted from me was to
be a sounding board for her voice, chattering
on and on about trivial things. I feel angry—
and I feel guilty for resenting her.
Lord, thank You that You always listen to me.
Lead me to a friendship that will
provide an equal give-and-take.

Unforgiveness

And Jesus said, Father, forgive them;
for they know not what they do.

LUKE 23:34 ASV

It's not always easy to forgive. If we are Christ's followers, however, we must follow His example. If He could forgive the people who were killing Him, we can certainly find a way to forgive those who hurt us!

Ultimately, when we can't forgive, we hurt ourselves more than anyone. Nursing a grudge damages our own hearts. It can even make us physically ill.

God wants to set us free from old grievances and harbored resentments. He will heal our wounded hearts and give us the strength to forgive. After all, He forgave us, didn't He?

Lord Jesus, if You could forgive the people who
stripped You and drove nails through Your hands
and feet, who hung You up on the cross to die,
then I know You can help me forgive those who
have offended or wronged me.

God, free me of resentment and
self-righteousness. Take the two-by-four
out my own eye before I worry too much
about the speck in someone else's!
Make me humble enough to forgive.

Jesus, in the Gospels, You always showed mercy to the sinners. But You had no patience for the proud and unforgiving Pharisees.

Lord, may I carry Your forgiveness to all who have hurt me. May they see You in me. Work Your reconciliation through me.

God, I know You want me to live at peace
with others—but I won't be able to do that until
I can forgive. Help me forgive that which seems
unforgiveable. Free my heart so that I can
be at peace with everyone.

Violence

Jesus said, "Put your sword back where it belongs. All who use swords are destroyed by swords."

MATTHEW 26:52 MSG

By our own standards, Peter would have been perfectly justified in using his sword to defend Jesus. But Christ calls us to a different standard. One of our greatest challenges as His followers is to walk His path of peace in the midst of a violent world.

Violence bombards us from all directions. It comes at us on the news, in movies, and on television. Violence touches our schools and our workplaces. We see it on our highways, we run into it in stores. It's evident at the national global level—and it even comes into our homes.

We may think we have no part in this violence, but Jesus calls us to examine our hearts. He reminds us that if our thoughts are full of rage and hatred, then we, too, nurse the roots of violence inside our very beings. He asks us instead to become His hands and feet on this earth, spreading His peace.

Lord, make me an instrument of Your peace. Where there is hatred, let me sow love. Where there is injury, pardon. Where there is doubt, faith. Where there is despair, hope. Where there is darkness, light. Where there is sadness, joy. O Divine Master, grant that I may not so much seek to be consoled, as to console. To be understood, as to understand, to be loved as to love. For it is in giving that we receive, it is pardoning that we are pardoned, and it is in dying that we are born to eternal life (Prayer of Francis of Assisi).

Jesus, You left Your peace with us. The peace
You give is not like the world's. We don't need
to be worried or afraid. We need never
resort to violence (John 14:27).

Lord, I believe that if I'm in Christ, I'm a new
creation. The old things have passed away and all
things have become new (2 Corinthians 5:17). Take all
violent thoughts away from me.
Make me a new creature.

If I have bitter envy and self-seeking in my heart, Lord,
You tell me that I am lying against Your truth. This is not
Your way of doing things, but the world's. For when envy
and self-seeking fill my heart, I have opened the door to
confusion and violence. Your way of doing things is far
different! It's based on peace and gentleness. When I do
things Your way, I'm willing to yield my way to another's;
I'm full of mercy for everyone; I don't show favoritism;
and I'm free of hypocrisy. The fruit of Your righteousness
is sown in peace when I become
Your peacemaker (James 3:14–18).

Father, when I realize that *violence* and *violation* have the same roots, I understand better how careful I need to be to walk Your path of peace. Any time I violate another's trust, whenever I trespass on another's rights, I am committing a form of violence. Make me careful to always treat others with Your respect.

Jesus, when I look at the world, I feel helpless to counteract the violence I see everywhere. But let me take the first step: I give You my own heart to change. Take out the greed and bitterness and unforgiveness I hold inside. Fill me instead with peace, goodwill, and kindness for everyone. May I, like Your cousin John, prepare the way of the Lord.

Weakness

*But those who trust in the LORD will find new
strength. They will soar high on wings like eagles.
They will run and not grow weary.
They will walk and not faint.*

ISAIAH 40:31 NLT

There are so many demands on our strength. So many crises to confront, so many problems to solve, so many people who need our help. We feel exhausted. We're not sure we can go on. Some days, we'd like to just give up. We've reached the end of our strength.

But when we acknowledge our own weakness, that's the moment when the Holy Spirit can begin to work in our lives in new ways. When we throw up our own hands, God's hands have room to work.

Lord, You know how weak I am. But I can do all things through You who gives me strength (Philippians 4:13).

Heavenly Father, make me strong in You. May my strength come from Your might (Ephesians 6:10).

Lord Jesus Christ, King of kings, You have power over life and death. You know even things that are uncertain and obscure, and our very thoughts and feelings are not hidden from You. Cleanse me from my secret faults. . . . You know how weak I am, both in soul and in body. Give me strength, O Lord, in my frailty and sustain me in my sufferings. Grant me a prudent judgment, dear Lord, and let me always be mindful of Your blessings (Ephrem of Syria).

I arise today
Through the strength of heaven....
I arise today
Through God's strength to pilot me;
God's might to uphold me,
God's wisdom to guide me,
God's eye to look before me,
God's ear to hear me,
God's word to speak for me,
God's hand to guard me,
God's way to lie before me,
God's shield to protect me,
God's hosts to save me...
Afar and anear,
Alone or in a multitude....

Christ shield me today. . .
Against wounding. . .
Christ with me, Christ before me,
Christ behind me, Christ in me,
Christ beneath me, Christ above me,
Christ on my right, Christ on my left,
Christ when I lie down, Christ when I sit down,
Christ in the heart of everyone who thinks of me,
Christ in the mouth of everyone who speaks of me,
Christ in the eye that sees me,
Christ in the ear that hears me.
I arise today
Through the mighty strength. . .
Of the Creator of creation
(Prayer of Saint Patrick).

Worry

*Don't worry about anything; instead,
pray about everything. Tell God what you need,
and thank him for all he has done.*

<small>PHILIPPIANS 4:6 NLT</small>

All of us worry. We worry about the future. We worry about our weight. We worry about our family. We worry about money. We worry about work responsibilities. Worry, worry, worry! The list of worries is endless.

Guess what the Old German root word of *worry* is? It's "to strangle"! Worries strangle us. They make it so we can't breathe in the Spirit of God. They twist our minds out of the healthy shape God wants them to have. Worries interfere with the flow of God's life into ours.

But our worries can be turned into prayers. Each time a worry occurs to us, we need to form the habit of lifting it up to God. As we offer our worries to Him, they will lose their stranglehold on our lives. And then we will find ourselves instead thanking God for all He has done.

Because I dwell in the secret place of the Most High, Lord, I shall abide under the shadow of the Almighty. You are my refuge and my fortress, my God. In You I will trust. You have delivered me from all of life's snares and dangers. You have covered me with Your feathers and under Your wings I take refuge. Your truth is my shield. I do not need to worry in the night, nor do I need to fret about dangers during the day. Neither sickness nor destruction are my concern. Even though people all around me are in trouble, I still don't need to worry, because You are my refuge. You—the Most High—are my dwelling place. You have given Your angels the job of looking after me. No matter what dangers I face, I am safe. Because of Your love, You will deliver me. You will set me in a high place. When I call on You, You answer me. If trouble comes, You will still be with me. You will deliver me and honor me. You will show me Your salvation all through my life. So why should I worry (Psalm 91)?

Lord, You are in complete control—
and You are greater than any of my worries.
I cannot change the future, I cannot change
human hearts, I may not be able to change the
circumstances of my life—so worrying is simply
a waste of time and energy! Teach me that my
energy could be better spent in prayer.

Thank You, Father, for giving me the confidence
that You are for me and with me. I know that life
holds nothing that You can't overcome. No power
is greater than You. I can rest in Your arms today,
knowing that You have everything under control.

Lord, I'm imagining that You are a mother hen,
and I'm a chick (Psalm 91:4). I've crawled under
Your wing. Your feathers are all around me.
I have nothing to worry about.

Loving Jesus, You know all the worries that flood
my thoughts. I feel helpless to stem their tide.
All I can do is ask You for help.

I realize, Lord, that when I worry, I'm trying to hold on to my own control over my life. I don't want to let go and accept that You may have other ideas. I want to make things happen the way I want them to happen. I don't trust You to be able to handle things on my own. It's as though You were carrying a suitcase that hardly weighed anything from Your perspective—and I was a little ant running alongside You, saying, "Let me carry it! I can carry it better! Let me! Let me!"

Lord, forgive me. I ask for Your will to be done in Your way in Your time. I trust You. I give You all my worries.